The Eagles of Hornby Island

Doug Carrick

Dedication

To Benn Kramer: The Eagle Man of Hornby Island

Benn Kramer holding eaglet.

The Eagles of Hornby Island

My Tree-top Neighbours

Douglas Carrick

hancock
house

ISBN 978-088839-649-5

Cataloguing in Publication Data

Carrick, Douglas
    The eagles of Hornby Island : my tree-top neighbours / Douglas Carrick.

ISBN 978-0-88839-649-5

1. Bald eagle—British Columbia—Hornby Island (Island).
2. Bald eagle—Behavior—British Columbia—Hornby Island (Island).
3. Bald eagle—Nests—British Columbia—Hornby Island (Island).
I. Title.

QL696.F32C36 2008   598.9'43097112   C2008-901412-X

Printed in Indonesia — TK PRINTING

Front cover photos: Screen shots from live wildlife cams.

We acknowledge the financial support of the Government of Canada through the Book Publishing Industry Development Program (BPIDP) for our publishing activities.

Published simultaneously in Canada and the United States by

HANCOCK HOUSE PUBLISHERS LTD.
19313 Zero Avenue, Surrey, B.C. Canada V3S 9R9
(604) 538-1114 Fax (604) 538-2262

HANCOCK HOUSE PUBLISHERS
1431 Harrison Avenue, Blaine, WA U.S.A. 98230-5005
(604) 538-1114 Fax (604) 538-2262

Website: **www.hancockhouse.com**
Email: **sales@hancockhouse.com**

Contents

Preface

When eagles are mentioned in this book, it always refers to "bald eagles" unless otherwise indicated. Their proper name is *Halaeetus leucocephalus,* from the four Greek words: *halos* (sea), *aetos* (eagle), *leukos* (white), and *kephalius* (head) — white-headed sea eagle. The common name, "bald eagle," is also a reference to a white-headed eagle, based on the old English word "balde," which meant "white."

Acknowledgements

I would like to thank all the people of Hornby Island who have kept me updated on the activities of our eagles — new nests, number of eaglets, dates of migration, dates of return, and especially unusual activities they observe. Much of my information has come from this source.

Above all, I appreciate how my wife, Sheila, encouraged me to proceed with this book. She knew that it meant a lot to me and backed me up completely. She went over every page with me, suggesting what should be added and what should be dropped and better ways of expressing it — a great partnership that will always be remembered and appreciated. We both hope the readers will enjoy the results.

Doug Carrick

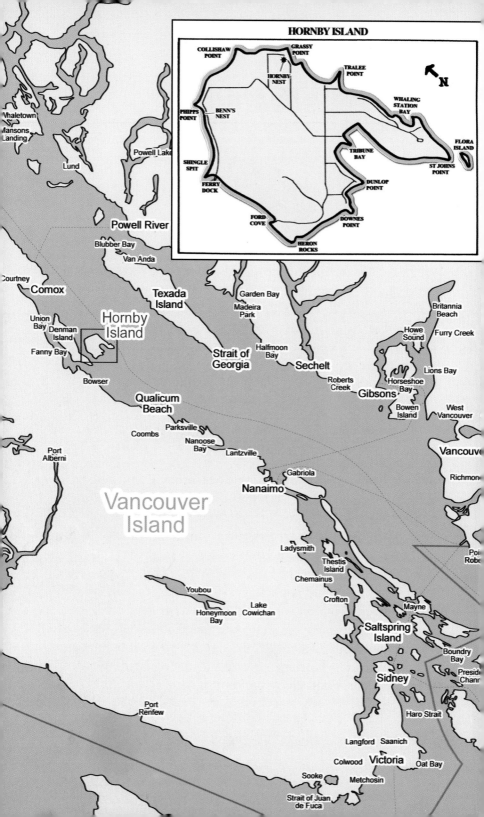

HORNBY ISLAND

COLLISHAW POINT
GRASSY POINT
TRALEE POINT
HORNBY NEST
WHALING STATION BAY
PHIPPS POINT
BENN'S NEST
FLORA ISLAND
SHINGLE SPIT
TRIBUNE BAY
ST JOHNS POINT
FERRY DOCK
DUNLOP POINT
FORD COVE
DOWNES POINT
HERON ROCKS

N

Whaletown
Mansons Landing
Lund
Powell Lake
Powell River
Blubber Bay
Van Anda
Courtney
Comox
Texada Island
Garden Bay
Madeira Park
Union Bay
Denman Island
Hornby Island
Fanny Bay
Halfmoon Bay
Strait of Georgia
Sechelt
Britannia Beach
Howe Sound
Furry Creek
Lions Bay
Horseshoe Bay
Roberts Creek
Gibsons
Bowser
Qualicum Beach
West Vancouver
Port Alberni
Parksville
Coombs
Nanoose Bay
Lantzville
Bowen Island
Vancouve
Richmon
Gabriola
Nanaimo
Vancouver Island
Ladysmith
Thestis Island
Poi
Robe
Chemainus
Youbou
Honeymoon Bay
Lake Cowichan
Crofton
Mayne
Saltspring Island
Boundry Bay
Sidney
Preside
Chann
Port Renfew
Haro Strait
Langford
Saanich
Colwood
Victoria
Oat Bay
Sooke
Metchosin
Strait of Juan de Fuca

Introduction

How It Began

Our house is located on the beach, in the center of the eagles' territory at Grassy Point on Hornby Island. We didn't plan it that way. It was the eagles that came to us. Eighteen years ago the eagles built a nest in the big tree behind our house, and a few months later fledged their first eaglet. Neither my wife nor I were birders at that time; but when an eagle enters your life it is hard to ignore, they are such impressive birds.

Mind you, their call isn't exactly impressive — a high, tinny *kee-kee-kee* — which can be heard for half a mile. It took a while to accept that a noble bird like an eagle could emit such a screechy sound, but over the years, I've grown to like it. One thing: you always know where they are.

One October, a friend, visiting for a few days, wondered where the eagles were. People visiting Hornby Island expect to see eagles. I explained that they were on migration and

Our house.

Looking east across the Georgia Strait towards Texada Island.

would return on October 2 (using the previous year's date of return). He immediately pointed out that it was already October 2. "Oh…then in the next few days," I said. About an hour later, the first eagle flew by the window. What timing! My friend was impressed, and I was impressed with my luck. I later learned that eagles do many things on schedule, but the date of return is one of the most consistent. Last year they did it again — returned on exactly that same date.

Before the eagles first arrived in this area, our main entertainment was watching George and the cormorants sitting on the Big Rock in front of our house. George is our neighbourhood gull, in his twentieth year of residence here. George and the cormorants seemed unconcerned when the eagles first built their nest, and unconcerned when the eagles perched in the Peters' tree, right above the Big Rock.

Unconcerned, perhaps, but forever vigilant. The moment the eagles fly from their perch, George and the cormorants also take to the air, determined never to be caught flat-footed. At the same time, the harlequin ducks scoot out to deeper water, ready to dive under. And the crows on the beach, the mallards in the Bay and the gulls on the Point, all become air-

Looking south at Sandstone Point and Tralee Point further south.

GRASSY POINT — BALD EAGLE TERRITORY

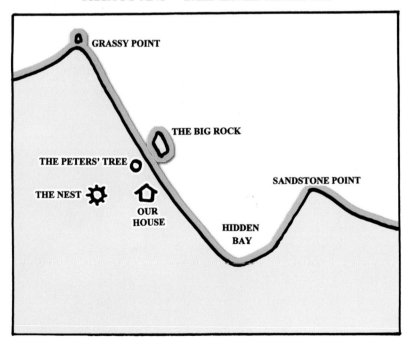

GRASSY POINT

THE BIG ROCK

THE PETERS' TREE

THE NEST

OUR
HOUSE

SANDSTONE POINT

HIDDEN
BAY

borne, none taking a chance of being attacked. Once in the air, smaller birds can usually outmanoeuvre larger ones. None want to be a "sitting duck."

We soon realized that the eagles had become the king and queen of the beach, with all other birds paying due respect. We tried to name them accordingly. We tried Elizabeth and Philip (after the monarchs of Britain), but that didn't seem to fit. The people in Britain don't run for their lives when Queen Elizabeth and Prince Philip drive by. So we tried more fearsome names like Attila and Genghis Khan, but they didn't sound right either. So, our eagles remained without names, identified only by their territory: the Grassy Point eagles. Many years later these same eagles starred on the Web Cam as the Eagles of Hornby Island.

George and the Cormorants

In front of our house is the Big Rock, surrounded by water at high tide and sitting high and dry at low tide. When we bought the property in 1980, we noticed all the cormorants stationed on the rock and a big white gull always sitting among them. Our good neighbour, Ken Peters, told us the gull's name was George. We soon talked of them as if they were a musical group — George and the Cormorants, the "Rock group."

George and the Cormorants.

They have a feeding relationship. From time to time, the cormorants leave the rock and dive down for herring and George paddles around waiting. The herring, frantically escaping the cormorants, swim to the surface and George gobbles them up as fast as he can. Having eaten their fill, George and the cormorants return to the rock and sit in blissful contentment. This cycle repeats itself several times a day.

One March, when the herring were spawning, a million gulls had arrived for the feast. Although the air was white with swirling gulls, George would allow none of them to land on the rock. He kept clearing the rock for three solid weeks until the multitude had dispersed. The next year was more of the same, with one exception. He allowed an attractive female, named Alice, to share his rock. They would feed together and rest together, thoroughly enjoying each other's company and thus became permanent partners, a relationship that lasted for many years.

George, Alice and the Cormorants.

Every morning we would wake up to see the two of them, George and Alice, sitting with the cormorants. And then one morning, there was only one gull. The other was down on the beech, trailing a wing behind. It was trying to fly to the rock, but toppled over with each attempt. Giving up, it worked its way to the water, swam south and was never seen again. No gull can survive an injured wing.

I began wondering which one it was, George or Alice? It's difficult to tell the difference — all glaucus-winged gulls look the same. Then I realized I could probably tell them apart by their behaviour. George was always completely at home with the cormorants, as if he had lived with them all his life (and perhaps he had). Alice, on the other hand, was uncomfortable with them. She wasn't that keen on her in-laws.

Close-up of a cormorant.

The Myth of George — Brought Up Like a Cormorant

I have made up a myth to explain George's close relationship with the cormorants. It's not true, but I still like it. It all began several years ago when I was walking along the bluffs of Helliwell Park. My friend John Badanic looked over the edge where the cormorants were nesting and noticed that gulls were nesting there also. Based on this experience, I imagined a mix-up of eggs, with a gull egg rolling into a cormorant nest where it hatched, was fed and brought up like a cormorant. He could fly as well as the other young cormorants but was unable to dive down for herring. But that didn't really matter. He would just float on the surface until the herring were driven up — ending up eating as much as the others. He grew up to be a strong and handsome gull.

Whatever the explanation, George fitted in with the cormorants but Alice did not. Often, when the cormorants got too close, she would tweak their feathers, making them jump. She would peck them and shove them, far more than was necessary. They were never aggressive with her, but she certainly was with them. With these things in mind, I looked again at the remaining gull. Was it George or Alice? Well, the answer was clear. The remaining gull was completely at home with the cormorants. There was no tweaking, pecking or shoving. It was George. And within a year or two, George had found another mate, whom we still call Alice, sometimes qualified as Alice II.

Harlequin Ducks

Other familiar neighbours on the beach are the harlequin ducks. They are small and brightly coloured, hence the name

Harlequin duck.

harlequin, defined as "a clown, usually dressed in garish colours". Although the least common of Canadian ducks, they are the most common around Hornby Island. A group of fifteen or so Harlequins station themselves on the rocky reef near the Big Rock — the same ducks year after year.

Eight years ago biologists began banding the harlequin ducks around Hornby Island, and volunteers were trained to record the numbers on the bands. We were asked to bring our telescopes to the opening session. A group of harlequins was sitting on the beach and we zoomed our telescopes onto their leg-bands. Soon I could hear, "It's A8, can you see it?" and others would reply, "Yes, and next to it is H3". Meanwhile, with my telescope, I couldn't even see the band, not to say the numbers on it. I felt like a kid with a plastic toy among adults with proper telescopes.

A couple of years later I purchased a much better telescope and have recorded a series of numbers that were repeated year after year. I have seen numbers "48" and "LF" for six years running. I have recorded "P3" on four different years, and "42" on three different years. There are others I have seen on two occasions but it is quite possible that they have been here on all six years and I have missed them. The same ducks come back year after year.

I am satisfied that the harlequins can be considered permanent residents of this territory, just as the eagles are, and just as George and the cormorants are. The same is true of the herons whose nesting site (heronry) is one mile south of us, and the hundred crows nesting behind us (to be discussed later), and a variety of other ducks, seals, sea lions, otters, mink, and many more creatures. They are all part of this wonderful fabric of life, sharing this same territory. The study of eagles is interrelated with all these other birds and creatures.

Eagles and Other Birds

Eagles and Ospreys

When we first bought our property in 1980, there were ospreys regularly patrolling the waters off our beach. Fishing one day in our little blue boat (eight feet long), I heard a great splash behind me. That was encouraging — a salmon jumping. I could see the ever-expanding rings in the water. And then, out of these rings emerged this large bird, with a salmon. What a sight! I realized it must be an osprey. I had heard about these birds and read about them, but this was the first time I had ever seen one in action. I became an "osprey man" overnight. They are interesting birds to watch. Every time they rise out of the water with a fish, they do two things: first, they shake off the water like a dog does to get rid of the excess weight; and, second, they spin the fish around so its head is facing forward, giving less air resistance in flight.

The ospreys were successful in catching a fish on 60 percent of their attempts. In later years, as the salmon became scarce, the percentage went way down. My interest in ospreys dropped when the eagles began nesting in the tree behind our house. Thinking about it later, I realized my waning interest in ospreys was simply because they weren't around any more. The eagles had displaced them. The two are not compatible. This became obvious one summer when an osprey was bold

Osprey.
Photo: Werner Eller

The eagle on its favourite perch, the Peters' Tree, above the Big Rock.
Photo: Dave Peters

When the eagle is away, the heron will play.

enough to fish directly in front of our house. It plunged into the water and came up with a fish, but both our eagles dove on it immediately, forcing it to drop the fish and make a hasty escape. There is just no point in fishing in eagle territory. In the last few years, only one osprey family has remained on Hornby Island.

Eagles and Herons

Great Blue Herons are another bird as large as eagles, with stilt-like legs, a long neck and a long pointed beak. They spend hours wading in shallow water, spearing small fish with their beaks. If disturbed, they let out agitated grunting noises, like a grumpy old man. They are immaculately clean; after swallowing a fish, they swish their beaks back and forth in the water until thoroughly clean. At their other end they are not so delicate. There is a general rule: never walk under a heron's nest without an umbrella.

For a large, lumbering bird, herons are amazingly manoeuvrable. I watched our two eagles dive down on a passing heron. It was like fighter planes attacking a bomber. My heart sank. The poor heron didn't have a chance. But at the last moment, the heron changed directions, and the eagles went whistling by, missing by five feet. They curved around for a second run, and then called it off. Herons aren't that easy to catch, so why bother?

The eagles had greater success on another occasion. Dante, across the island, told me about herons raiding her goldfish pond and how she had bought a life-sized plastic heron that she planted at the edge of the pond. Other herons stay clear, recognizing that the pond has already been claimed. Soon after, an eagle flew towards her property, closer and closer, and lower and lower. And it kept coming. It snapped up the plastic heron and flew towards the sea. Realizing its mistake, the eagle dropped the heron, and Dante was able to recover her precious guardian of the pond.

The herons had a large heronry at Tralee Point, a mile south of here. I visited it when it was at its peak in size — about 45 active nests. It sounded like a zoo. The young (up to four per nest) were screaming for food, especially when the parents arrived. The young by that time were as large as their parents and were savagely pushing and pecking each other in the battle for first feeding. The following year, the eagles began raiding these nests and took most of the young. After several years of this predation, the herons deserted this heronry and moved into two smaller breeding colonies in a densely forested area, but the eagles got them there as well. In recent years, many heronries around the Georgia Strait have been struggling for the same reason.

Many believe that the devastation of the heron colonies is related to the collapse of the Georgia Strait salmon stocks — that herons have become a substitute food for the eagles when they could no longer get salmon. Others think it is part of the long-term cycles of nature; recently the eagle population has gone up and the heron population down. There is a tendency to think of the recent heron population as being the "normal" balance. Standing back at a distance, however, there is another interpretation — that the recent heron populations have been abnormally high, because the eagle populations have been unnaturally low. In the 1960s and 1970s the eagles throughout North America were decimated by the use of DDT, allowing a population explosion of herons. Now that the eagles are recovering to their normal numbers, the herons are being reduced to their normal numbers.

But at what point in history do we arrive at the "normal" balance? Of course, the greatest imbalance of all is the population explosion of the human species, accompanied by the decimation of almost every other species in the world. The obvious answer would be to encourage birth control, but that appears to be a taboo topic, so I'm not even going to mention it!

Eagles and Turkey Vultures

In the summer there are almost as many turkey vultures on Hornby Island as bald eagles. After wintering in California and Mexico, the vultures arrive at Hornby in early April and stay until the end of September. Both eagles and vultures feed on carrion, but vultures are far superior at sniffing out dead animals. Several years ago a bear swam to Hornby Island and quickly developed a taste for sheep. It killed one on a neighbouring farm, and within two hours several vultures were circling overhead. Two days later, the bear killed another sheep on the other side of the island and the vultures were there also. In situations like this, the vultures are the "first responders," with the eagles providing later cleanup duties.

Since the eagles and vultures eat much of the same food, you would think there would be constant battles between the two, but this does not happen. One day a friend, Jack Hansed, asked me, "Who is tougher, an eagle or a vulture?" By the cunning smile on his face, I knew he had the answer. "The eagle, of course," I answered.

He explained that there was a dead seal on his beach. The vultures were feasting on the carcass and the eagles were standing around as onlookers. Obviously then, vultures are tougher.

Not wanting to accept this, I offered another interpretation (or rationalization). The eagles had probably been there first, and only after they had their fill did they step aside to let the vultures at it. Jack didn't accept this interpretation.

Two weeks later, I noticed one of our eagles perched in the Peters' Tree. I threw a fish on the beach below, but the eagle showed no interest. Then two vultures circled along the beach, getting closer and closer. Aha, I thought, I'll soon have proof of who is tougher. Both vultures landed next to the fish and began feeding. I couldn't believe it. "Are you going to put up with this?" I asked the eagle. "It's your fish, you know. It's your territory!" But, still no reaction. Oh dear! Will I have to confess this to Jack? Our eagle finally dropped down to the beach near the vultures and stepped forward. The vultures stepped back and flew away. All very delicately done — not an impressive show of dominance. Eagles and vultures seem to avoid a showdown, and the question, "Who is tougher?" has yet to be answered. (I still think that eagles are tougher.)

Eagles and Geese

Until recently there were few Canada geese around Hornby Island, but they have been on the increase. These tough and aggressive birds show little fear of eagles; I don't know why they are so bold. Their beaks seem more suitable for nipping grass than tearing flesh, and their feet seem more suitable for paddling in water — nothing like the eagles' sharp talons. I believe, however, that their wings can be formidable weapons, used for slashing karate chops. Whatever it is, the eagles pay them great respect. Geese will often swim within four or five feet of an eagle, not showing the least concern.

The geese have nests somewhere in Hidden Bay, to the right of our house. Early every summer, the geese come out of the bay showing off their new families. The male is in front, followed

Who's afraid of the big bad eagle?

closely by five or six goslings, and the female brings up the rear. In some years, there are several families making an appearance, but always in that same protective formation. There is still no hassle with the eagles as long as the family is healthy and intact.

One summer, one of the goslings was always straggling. Later, when the other goslings were learning to fly, this one was unable to do so. When the family flew to another part of the beach, it could only swim after them, arriving ten minutes later. After a few days, it was no longer seen. Although adult geese can defend themselves effectively, goslings are vulnerable. Every year, the eagles catch one or two goslings.

An unusual thing happened at Bradsdadsland, the home of Benn Kramer and his famous eagle nest. After using this nest for eight years, the eagles moved to a new nest further inland. I kept an eye on the abandoned nest, watching to see if such nests were ever re-occupied by the original family or by new families. Two years later, I spotted what looked like a Canada goose in the nest. I couldn't believe it. I thought that Benn Kramer had put a decoy in the nest for a joke, but was assured by others that it was a real goose. Then I saw Benn, who knew all about it. He explained that the Canada geese had used the nest the previous year also. But the nest is 80 feet above the ground. How do the goslings get down to the water? Benn explained that they tumble down from branch to branch and don't seem to get hurt. It was high tide when it happened, so they landed in the water. Once down, they never return to the nest.

I then did some research. According to statistics on coastal Canada geese, 64 percent nest on the ground, 13 percent in osprey or eagle nests, 11 percent on muskrat or beaver lodges, 9 percent on artificial nest tubs, and 3 percent on bridges or pilings. The maximum height for a goose in a tree nest was 100 feet. So, it wasn't all that unusual to find a goose in an eagle's nest.

A room with a view. *Photo: Benn Kramer*

The goose in the eagles' nest. *Photo: Benn Kramer*

Golden Eagles on Hornby Island?

Immature bald eagles come in various tones of brown and look similar to golden eagles. It is difficult to distinguish between the two. Despite the many reports of golden eagle sightings on Hornby Island, I think it has rarely happened. What complicates things even more is the common belief that golden eagles are larger than bald eagles. A report I often receive is, "It was much larger than a bald eagle, so it must be a golden eagle."

Peterson's *Field Guide to Western Birds* records both the length and wingspan of the bald eagle as larger than those of the golden eagle.

The *Sibley Guide to Birds* also shows the bald eagle as the larger bird. On the other hand, the National Geographic *Birds of North America* gives the edge to the golden eagle. In any case, the differences are not significant.

Here is information that might help in understanding eagles:

- Northern bald eagles (Alaska) are larger than BC bald eagles.
- Southern eagles (Florida) are smaller than BC eagles.
- Females are larger than males (an average of 11½ pounds for females against 9 pounds for males).
- Immature eagles are larger than mature eagles (their wing feathers are much longer, to assist their flight in early years).

To sum up, an immature female eagle will be significantly larger than a mature male. The largest eaglet ever fledged from our nest was a giant. We named her "Big Bertha." She spent a considerable time sitting on our skylights grabbing at bumblebees flying on the underside, needless to say, without success. Not only did she have the size advantage of being immature and a female, but there might also be another factor. For some time now, I have harboured secret thoughts (closeted until now) that she was the illegitimate child of a northern male. This too, would account for her magnificent size — but this is more imagination than science.

Golden eagles can be understood better by understanding their diet. They feed mainly on small mammals such as rabbits, mice, and ground squirrels, or in some areas, chipmunks, prairie dogs, and marmots. A rancher in Alberta told me that golden eagles make an appearance every time he plows, chasing down the mice dug out of their homes. To catch these small mammals, the golden eagles first have to see them, and then catch them. This requires open prairies, deserts or mountains, all having sparse vegetation. The dense underbrush of the Pacific coast hardly allows a clear sighting and provides many hidey-holes for the prey to escape — not a suitable terrain for golden eagles and not a place you are likely to find them.

There is one habitat, not so far away from Hornby Island, that is suitable for golden eagles — the mountains of Vancouver

Island. Golden eagles regularly patrol Green Mountain, Mount Arrowsmith, Mount Washington and adjacent peaks, watching for the rare and endangered Vancouver Island marmots. No sooner had biologists reintroduced replacement marmots to the wild than they were eaten up by golden eagles, with assistance from wolves and cougars. The tide has been turned in favour of the marmots now that guards are stationed on the mountains to frighten away these predators.

One September, my wife and I took a special trip covering the southern part of Saskatchewan (the Cyprus Hills), the foothills of Alberta and the drier parts of British Columbia — all golden eagle territory. We visited museums, bird rescue centers, wildlife refuges, government wildlife offices, and a taxidermist, thus becoming instant experts, at least on stuffed golden and bald eagles. Sixteen of the eagles we saw were mounted and the two live ones might as well have been stuffed — they didn't move once during our visit.

I think I can now recognize a golden eagle, and believe that I have not seen a golden eagle on Hornby Island. The ones that appear to be golden eagles are really immature female bald eagles (maybe with a bit of northern blood).

Early Observations

Establishing Territories

The peace of our area was disturbed when the eagle family just south of us, the "Nomads," moved their nest closer to our eagles' territory. The Nomads, as you can guess, were always changing nests, but this time came a little too close. The eagles on both sides screeched at each other and dove at each other with talons outstretched, but it was all "sound and fury" — the process of establishing new boundaries. No physical contact occurred, and in due time a boundary was accepted by both sides.

GRASSY POINT

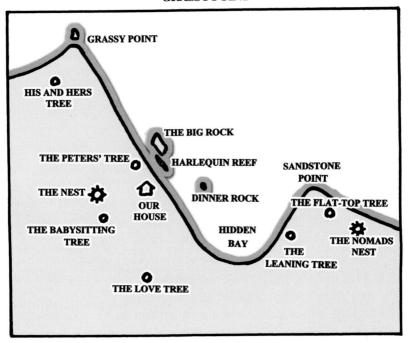

Our eagles' territory extends south to the "Leaning Tree" on Sandstone Point and the Nomads' territory begins with the next tree, the "Flat-top Tree." To the north, our eagles' territory extends to the "His and Hers Tree" on Grassy Point, a boundary never seriously contested since the next family is quite a distance away.

A little cheating occurs from time to time. Once I saw the two eagles from the Flat-top Tree dive-bombing a flock of wigeons in Hidden Bay (our territory). Ducks and feathers were flying everywhere. One of our eagles decided to join the melee. With wings flapping double speed and on a downhill path, it was flying at an incredible speed. As our eagle reached the bay, a wigeon broke from the clutches of the other eagles, but right into the talons of our eagle. It circled back towards the Big Rock with the wigeon in tow, but the other eagles weren't having any of it. They had done all of the work; it was their wigeon and they were determined to get it back. One of them caught up and hooked into the wigeon with one talon. Immediately both eagles spun out of control and plummeted to the water, still clutching the wigeon between them. The ensuing struggle was brief. The neighbouring eagle retreated and our eagle got the wigeon.

There are eighteen bald eagle pairs on Hornby Island, each pair claiming its own territory, meaning there are eighteen boundaries, each a potential war-zone. But all in all, compared with humans, territorial fighting is not a big item in the lives of eagles. In the year of writing this book, the nations of the world spent one thousand million dollars on military preparation (which is all about defending or attacking territories). Even peace-loving United States spends 19 percent of its federal budget on the military. I don't suppose the eagles spend as much as one percent of their energies over territorial disputes. I feel eagles have been much maligned as symbols of warfare. They are gentle doves compared with humans. Eagles are more civilized; they negotiate their differences mainly by screeching.

The Drowning Eagle

Soon after the eagles first nested behind our house, I saw one of them flying towards shore with a salmon; but it was losing altitude rapidly and splashed into the water 300 feet from shore. I nearly panicked, fearing it would drown. What to do? I had to be quick. I had a little blue boat on the beach and could row out to the eagle. But how do you lift a frantic eagle from the water (sharp beak and talons) without being torn to shreds? I checked the eagle again with my binoculars. Instead of floundering in the water as I expected, it was swimming to shore, with regular overhand strokes and was quite comfortable in the water. Everything was under control. It lifted both wings from the water, reached forward, and then stroked through the water, over and over, with the salmon in tow. After thirty strokes, it let go the salmon and flew directly out of the water to a perch tree. It was not the disaster I had expected — no big deal at all.

A year later, seeing something splashing off shore, I looked in the telescope. It was another eagle swimming, this time way out. Realizing it had a long way to go, I began counting strokes and recorded its time in the water — 250 strokes and 21 minutes in the water. This was in February and the water was icy cold. I thought the eagle would collapse upon reaching shore, but it didn't. It immediately dragged the salmon up the beach, flew with it to a large rock and proceeded with dinner. The salmon must have weighed close to four pounds. Other similar cases will come up as the book continues, but these were my first two experiences showing that eagles are good swimmers and are fully at ease in the water.

Not entirely a land bird.

The Non-retractable Talons

Myths didn't die off with the ancient Greeks. They are with us today, and several are related to eagles. The first one told to me was about eagles having non-retractable talons. It tells of an eagle latching its talons into the back of a large salmon. The salmon dove down, taking the eagle with it, and because the eagle could not release its talons, it was drowned.

Hearing this story repeatedly, I began asking the person telling the story if he had seen this himself. "No, I heard this from so and so". To this day, I have not met a person who has actually seen this happen and I suspect that, in fact, it never has happened. It's just a myth, a story people find fascinating and love to repeat. A bit like one of Aesop's fables, illustrating what happens to greedy little boys.

Just think about it. If this story were true, there wouldn't be an eagle alive today. They would have become extinct long ago, all pulled under water and drowned. But you don't have to think. Just open your eyes and look. I've seen many eagles swimming home the fish. The first one, already related, swam with the salmon for thirty strokes and then, yes, let go. And many more have brought salmon to shore, let go their talons and proceeded to eat the salmon. There is absolutely no problem in retracting their talons. As mentioned, nobody I know of has seen otherwise.

But this story will be around for many years to come. Not long ago a group of us were visiting a bird sanctuary. The guide provided much interesting information about the birds but saved the best part for the end — the story about the eagles' non-retractable talons. It's a memorable story, and people just love it.

The Duck Episode

The next significant event in my early eagle observations was related to a duck feeding on the beach. I think it was a mallard, but its feathers were in such poor condition it was difficult to tell. It looked very unhealthy and I wondered why it was alone. You don't often see ducks by themselves. They are generally in small groups, if not in larger flocks. Perhaps it was old and unable to keep up with the others. As I was pondering these things, it suddenly took off and flew to the sea where it landed. Our eagle was swooping down from above. I was almost screaming, "Dive under! Dive under!" At the last split second, it did go under, just avoiding the eagle's talons. And the moment the eagle flew by, it popped up again.

The eagle circled for a second run at the duck, then a third run, and a fourth run. Each time the duck waited for the last split second before ducking down. It was unnerving to watch. The timing was so close. On the fifth run the eagle again missed the duck but the eagle's mate was immediately behind it and grabbed the duck the moment it popped up.

The eagle then swam the duck to shore and dragged it up the beach.

The next part I really didn't want to watch. Would it start tearing the duck apart alive, or what? The eagle just stood on the duck's chest. The duck was able to breath out but with the weight on its chest, was unable to breath in again. After several breaths out and none going in, the duck became still.

Then began the plucking. Holding the duck with its talons, the eagle pulled the feathers with its beak, tossing them up in the air. In no time the beach was blanketed with feathers. And the meal began. In this case, it didn't last long. Several other eagles arrived wanting to share the feast, forcing the eagle to escape with the duck. It flew to Sandstone Point with several eagles following and then turned back again, still followed by one pesky immature eagle.

The eagle's mate came to the rescue. It flew down on the young eagle with talons extended. Just before contact, the immature eagle flipped over on its back, grasping the oncoming talons. The two eagles went into a spin, plummeting down, head over tails, but released talons before hitting the ground. The immature eagle flew away and our eagle finished its meal with no further interruptions.

Some observations:

- The prey of eagles is generally old, very young, injured or ill, and, more often than not, dead (carrion). In this case, it was old.
- If they could catch the young and healthy, there would soon be none left.
- Eagles often work in pairs.
- Immature eagles are more likely than adults to attempt scrounging food from others.
- The eagles' best defence, when attacked by talons, is to grasp the talons — very common among eagles and nearly always ending in a free-fall.

Diving Ducks and Dabblers

Most of the ducks seen around Hornby Island are diving ducks, such as the harlequins. They can swim underwater easily and can stay down for a minute or longer. One January, when our eagle must have been hungry, it made a concerted attack on a group of swimming harlequin ducks. It first separated one from the others, perhaps one that appeared weaker, and swooped down on it. The duck plunged under and the eagle flew to where the duck might surface. The duck popped up for a gasp of air and ducked down again, with the eagle flying after it. This repeated over and over. Sometimes the eagle was far from the spot the duck surfaced and at other times it was right above it, forcing the harlequin to dive again without a proper breath. For a while it looked as if the eagle was going to wear the duck down. I was getting worried. After fifteen such attempts, the eagle gave up the chase, having burnt much energy with no results. The eagle was young and foolish at that time, and I have never seen it attempting to catch a harlequin since. Diving ducks are most difficult to catch.

Dabbling ducks are different. They are the ones, sometimes called "puddle ducks," seen in great numbers on lakes, ponds and in parks. They feed in shallow water, simply dipping their heads down with their tails going up, resulting in another name, "bums-up" ducks. We have only two types of dabbling ducks around Hornby Island, mallards and American wigeons. The problem with dabblers is that they cannot dive down and swim underwater to escape predators. This was the problem with the old mallard, previously discussed. When frightened enough, they can get under water for a second or two but bounce right up again, like a cork.

Having this weakness, you would wonder that there are any dabblers left in the world; they would all have been caught by eagles thousands of years ago. So why are there so many around? I think it must be because of their instant take-off abilities. They can fly right out of the water at a steep angle, almost straight up, like a helicopter. Once airborne, as mentioned earlier, most smaller birds can out-fly or out-manoeuvre eagles.

My conclusion is that this particular mallard was caught, not just because it couldn't dive under as diving ducks do, but also because it was too old for instant take-off and strong flight as in its younger days. Only in desperation did it try diving down, and it didn't succeed.

Fighting Eagles

From time to time eagles fight each other. The aggressive eagle dives with talons thrust out and attempts to skewer the other's back. At the last second, the eagle being attacked flips over and grasps the talons of the upper eagle. They tumble down in an uncontrolled spin, but before hitting the ground, they let go and fly their own ways. This is the typical fight among eagles, short and sweet, and without serious consequences.

In one case, however, two fighting eagles tumbled down but were so late in unlocking talons they both hit the ground. One recovered and flew away, but the other was taken to a bird rescue center where it died. On another occasion, the fighting eagles hit a branch of a tree, one eagle dangling down on each side of the branch, but still grasping talons. They hung there for half an hour, neither willing to disengage. The tree-climber was called to the rescue and just as he arrived, the eagles let go, tumbled towards the ground and flew away.

There are fights that are horrible to watch. Two eagles locked talons in front of our house and tumbled into the sea. They sparred with their beaks and they slashed with their wings. After giving out a great mauling, the dominant eagle held the other's head under water. All I could see was a white tail above water. Somehow the weaker eagle got its head up but twice more it was dunked under. "Oh no! It may be one of our eagles," I thought. Maybe this is how vigorous young eagles take over the territory of older eagles.

Then the tougher eagle let go, lifted out of the water and flew away. The defeated eagle was still alive. It attempted to fly but was too exhausted. It started to swim and went in circles, as if one wing was injured, but it finally straightened out and got to shore. It rested for 10 minutes, and then flew away. I was so pleased that it survived. At the same time, I was concerned. If it was one of our eagles, it no longer seemed capable of defending its territory.

Soon after, I spotted our own two eagles sitting side by side on their favourite perch, not a feather out of place. Neither of them was involved in the fight, thank goodness, and they are managing quite well to this day.

After this experience I was at least half-prepared for the next event a few months later. The phone rang and a desperate voice told me that one eagle was killing another eagle at Grassy Point. Grabbing a towel and gloves I dashed to the Point. A group of people told me, "One eagle is killing another," pointing along the beach. The next group exclaimed the same and pointed further along the beach. Finally a woman and her daughter pointed into the bush. A very beaten up eagle was sitting on a stump. They had chased away the aggressor eagle.

The woman was really shaken by the savage beating she had witnessed. "That big eagle was such a bully", she repeated over and over. "Well," I explained, "the big eagles are generally the females. The smaller one in the bush is probably a male." Her face lit up. "Oh, that's OK then," and joyfully added, "He probably deserved it."

Bath Time for Eagles

I have never seen eagles having a bath in our area, but Jan Bevan assured me that eagles do have baths. Every year, she told me, eagles gather in great numbers for a bath in the beaver pond, near her house. But this occurs only in herring season (March).

Last herring season (2007), the eagles were bathing at Olsen's farm. We had so much rain that the farm had more ponds and puddles than grass. I counted almost 100 eagles enjoying their baths — dunking and splashing, flapping their wings and generally having a good time. Similar reports came from other parts of the island. In every case, however, the bathing was done during herring season.

My explanation for this goes back many years. Growing up, I used to swim in both lakes and the sea. I always preferred the sea because I floated higher in the water, and also I could comb my hair once and it would stay put for the rest of the day. The salty water cemented my hair nicely in place. Our towels also got stiff as boards.

Perhaps this is what the eagles don't like about salty water, and are trying to wash it off. While dunking for herring, they get far more salt water on them than at any other time of the year and therefore have a greater need to wash it off. So it seems logical that herring time is also bath time for the eagles.

Dangers Faced by Eagles

Falling Nests

When a nest falls out of the tree, it is fatal to young chicks. Sometimes this happens because of poor construction. For example, one family of eagles two miles south of us, which I call the "Dysfunctional" family, had several nests fall down, with the loss of several chicks. They had great difficulty in building stable nests. However, even well built nests can be blown down in a storm. Last spring, two nests were blown down in Victoria and four chicks died.

Falling Out of Nests

When the chicks are almost grown they clamber onto the edges of their nests, and sometimes fall out. Benn Kramer, of Bradsdadsland, found one of his eaglets at the base of the tree. He placed it in a backpack, climbed the tree and returned it to the nest. In doing so, the other eaglet in the nest was startled and fell out, tumbling a quarter the way down before grasping a branch. Benn retrieved that one too and placed it back with the first one. It was a dramatic event, watched by a hundred campers below, some with video cameras. Both eaglets were successfully fledged a few weeks later.

Most eaglets falling out of nests, however, don't have a hero to rescue them. What is their fate? By the time they venture to the edge of the nest, they can flutter to the ground without injury, but are unable to fly back up. In one case, the parents continued to feed the eaglet on the ground (with the help of everyone in the neighbourhood) and the eaglet, somewhat slowly, learned to fly and belatedly went on migration.

Other eaglets may not be so fortunate. Friends of ours, on the other side of the island, found an eaglet on the beach that had not been fed. They took it in their car across the two ferries to the Mountainaire Avian Rescue Society on Vancouver Island. The eaglet was terribly light in weight, obviously suffering from starvation, and it was crawling with lice. Soon my friends were crawling with lice, and so was their car. They are no longer keen on bird rescues. This eaglet did not survive.

I was phoned about another eaglet that had fallen from its nest. While walking along the beach to that location, I pondered what to do with the eaglet – to take it to a bird rescue center or leave it for nature to take its course? When I spotted the grounded bird, it was the sickliest thing you could ever imagine. Instead of having brown feathers speckled with white, this one's feathers were grey. Instead of bright yellow feet, they also were grey. It had no feathers on its head and its nostrils seemed deformed. I could look right through its nostrils to the other side. I decided then and there — no point in rescuing this one; it's not fit for survival. Then I looked up. Circling above were two worried parents. Vultures! It wasn't a sickly eaglet, but a perfectly healthy young vulture.

Humans Inadvertently Harming Eagles

Humans can inadvertently harm eagles. For example, our power lines cause a significant number of injuries and deaths each year, either by the eagles flying into them or by electrocution. When these things occur with any frequency, our power authority, BC Hydro, responds accordingly. Power lines having had frequent collisions are equipped with bright markers. In one case, the power line was relocated. Electrocutions can be averted by spacing the lines more than six and a half feet apart, the wingspan of eagles. It is only when an eagle touches both wires that the electricity shorts through its body.

Cars occasionally hit eagles, usually when the eagles are attracted to road-kill (on Hornby, usually deer or opossums). This is especially a problem if several eagles are fighting over the carrion, distracting them from oncoming traffic. The Hornby Island road crews remove all carcasses to the gravel pit, where the eagles can feed in safety.

In agricultural areas, the greatest risk to eagles is from pesticides. In the Fraser Valley, farmers were treating their fields with pesticide pellets to protect their potatoes against a wireworm. Ducks ate the pellets and died. Eagles, in turn, ate the ducks and also died. The pesticides were powerful but short-lived, so would be of no danger for later human consumption, but the ducks and eagles didn't wait the prescribed time.

Poisonings such as these are being monitored constantly by a variety of government agencies that recommend (and insist on) alternative pest controls. As a result, the number of eagle poisonings has been dramatically reduced in recent years. Because eagles are such noticeable birds, people soon report if anything is wrong. Thus, eagles, like canaries in coalmines, have become an early warning of ecological problems.

Humans Intentionally Harming Eagles

Humans can intentionally harm eagles. Fifty years ago, some people would shoot eagles just for target practice (the wild west), but those days are gone. The State of Alaska had a bounty on eagles until 1953. People were paid $2 per bird, in the belief that eagles were depleting the salmon stocks — never true at any time. Eagles certainly feed on salmon carcasses after they are spawned out, occasionally catch an injured salmon floundering near the surface, but rarely catch a healthy salmon. But this is all past history. Eagles are no longer shot for sport or for bounties. In fact they are protected everywhere in North America, and the eagle population is rebounding accordingly.

Despite the laws protecting eagles, and despite the severity of the penalties for breaking these laws, a disturbing thing occurred in February 2005. Forty-eight eagle carcasses were found in North Vancouver, with heads, talons and large feathers removed for sale to the lucrative (but illegal) eagle-parts market in the United States and elsewhere. This caused enormous pub-

lic outrage, and the police received 120 tips about the culprits. As a result, more than a dozen people were charged and will be brought to trial in due time.

Conservation officers have pointed out that these forty-eight carcasses are just the tip of the iceberg. It has been estimated that anywhere from 500 to 1,000 eagles annually have been poached in recent years. Horrible as poaching is, it is nowhere near as bad as the continuing loss of environment. Given time, the eagles will repopulate the areas affected by the illegal poaching, but if the eagles lose their environment, it is gone forever. If you are upset at the poaching, you should be far more upset about the degradation of the environment, not just for the eagles, but for yourselves also. People are now well aware of this.

A large illegal eagle parts market occur in the southwestern United States.
Photos: Kay Johnston from Spirit of Powwow

Eagle Nests

Locations

On the map below, are the locations of all thirty-six eagle nests that I have known over the last eighteen years. Most of them are no longer being used, and a number of them have since fallen from the trees. They are numbered in clockwise order starting at the ferry dock and working around the island. I have named each nest, sometimes after the geographic location, sometimes after the nearest road and sometimes after the nearest people.

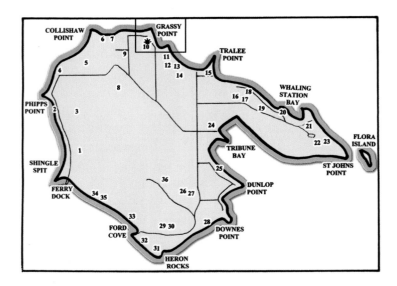

For example, nest #1 is the "Shire" nest, named after the large property where it is located. Nest #2 is the "Bradsdadsland" nest, which could also be spelled Brad's Dad's Land. It is named after the campsite at that location, made famous in Canada by the late Benn Kramer, who will be discussed later.

Nest #3 is where the Bradsdadsland eagles moved to, after eight years in nest #2, their original location. Nest #4 is the

"Trimbles' Corner" nest, a new one built early in 2006. These newcomers fledged no offspring that year (as is often the case in the first year of eagle nesting), but have been guarding their nest over the winter and will probably try again this year. This is the most visible nest on the island, just 20 feet from the road; you don't have to leave your car to see it.

Without going over each of the thirty-six nests, I'll just point out two others. More people have seen the "Helliwell Park" nest, #23, than any other nest. It is one of the largest nests on the island, and most likely the oldest (from reports of old-timers). It is also beautifully shaped, like a bowl. And nest #10 is the one behind my house near Grassy Point. It is the nest I have been watching for eighteen years, and the nest seen on the webcam by millions of people around the world.

Big Trees Preferred

Eagles prefer big trees for their nests. All the nests on Hornby Island are built in old growth or first growth Douglas firs. These were already large trees at the time of Captain Cook's first exploration of the British Columbia coast in 1778. The largest tree on Hornby Island (no nest) is along the Rainforest Trail. It is twenty-five feet in circumference, and four men can just barely reach around it. The largest trees having eagle nests are listed in order below, skipping a number of moderate sized trees, and then listing the two smallest trees:

#15 Tralee Point	23 feet around (See page 44)
#5 Collishaw Point	22½ feet
#29 Euston Road	22½ feet
#24 Tribune Bay	19 feet
#22 Helliwell Junction	18½ feet
#10 Grassy Point	18 feet
#23 Helliwell Park	13½ feet
#2 Bradsdadsland	11 feet

The largest eagle nest tree at Tralee Point, #15, twenty-three feet in circumference.

The Tralee Point tree is truly a giant, and the amazing thing is that it is still growing taller. The Collishaw Point tree was even taller when I first spotted it from Mount Geoffery. It towered above all surrounding trees. An eagle was sitting on top. Down forty feet was a nest, built in the first available branches. These eagles fledged an eaglet in 1998 and another in 1999, but the following winter the top fifty feet broke off, including the nest. Early the next spring the eagles built a new nest fifteen feet further down and in 2000 fledged another eaglet, and two more in 2001. Then, another twenty-five feet broke off, including the nest, and the eagles finally abandoned this tree. This is typical of the way old growth firs die off, working from the top down, section by section, a process taking hundreds of years.

Eagles prefer these larger trees because they are steadier in windstorms than the smaller second-growth trees. In severe storms the tops of second-growth trees are bent over almost parallel with the ground — rather frightening if you are under them, and worse if you are up there in a nest. A bit like the nursery rhyme:

When the wind blows, the cradle will rock, ...
And down will come baby, cradle and all.

The eagles know all about that. Another reason for the larger trees is that their branches are strong enough to support the weight of the nests, which can be as heavy as a small car.

After having been logged for 100 years, it is amazing that there are any first-growth trees left on Hornby Island. I asked Ron Dalziel, an old-timer, about this. He had logged over the Grassy Point area with his father almost sixty years ago. "They had conk", he explained. "Why cut them down, drag them to the sea and tow them to a saw mill only to be told they are no good?" Such trees have been infected with a fungal disease, which weakens the structure of the wood. The loggers can see which ones are infected by the bracket fungus (conks) growing out of their bark.

Ron added, "We didn't even cut them down. The trunks and branches would just junk up the ground, making it difficult to drag out the good timber. We just left them standing where they were, out of the way." And to this day, most of those "conky" trees are still standing, not good for lumber, but excellent for eagles' nests.

Waterfront Properties Preferred

Glancing at the map (page 42), it is obvious that eagles prefer waterfront properties, and why not? That's where most of their food comes from. Sixteen of the Hornby Island nests are within 400 feet of the water and another eight are in the next 400 feet (semi-waterfront). This belt along the beach is where the eagles prefer to build their nests, but suitable trees are not always available. For example, the first two miles from the ferry is all farmland, with few trees. The Bradsdadsland nest #2 and the Trimbles' Corner nest #4 are the only trees near the sea that are suitable for nests. When the Bradsdadsland eagles decided to change nests (as they do from time to time), they had to go across the farmland to the next nearest tree #3, now 2,400 feet from the sea. Also because of the farmland, the Shire nest #1 had to be located 2,000 feet from the sea.

Keeping these things in mind, nest # 8 baffles me. It is 4,600 feet from the nearest beach, by far the greatest distance of all the nests. I had heard about this nest years ago, but never checked it out, mainly because I didn't believe an eagle's nest could exist so far from the sea. Anyway, I finally did check it and found it to be a dandy big nest. But it still baffles me. Why are they so far from the sea? Why aren't they like normal eagles? There must be some explanation, I'm sure. I might point out that nest #26 is a bit deviant also at 3,300 feet from the sea.

The concern about these longer distances is the amount of

energy burnt to fly food to the nest, especially as the eaglets grow larger, consuming ever-greater quantities of food. In addition, the further the nest is from the sea, the higher up it is in elevation. Flying uphill with a weight is much more difficult than flying level. For these reasons, eagles tend to nest close to the sea whenever possible.

Nest Building

After returning from migration in October, the eagles start their first phase of nest building, adding up to ten branches a day to their nest. By mid-November it is getting colder and the eagles need more food to stay warm. At the same time, the daylight hours are getting shorter, so the eagles stop bringing branches to the nest and concentrate on seeking food. Throughout December and January, it is food only. In February, however, they start the second phase of nest building and continue on adding more branches, twigs and dry grass until the eggs are laid at the end of March. Instead of being in two stages, I now think of nest building as being one continuous period from mid-October to late March, merely interrupted by winter.

Home Sweet Home.

Most nest building is simply making additions to already existing nests — more like doing renovations. Sometimes, however, it means starting an entirely new nest and it is surprising how rapidly this occurs, especially when you see the size of a new nest.

We had a rare chance to see a new nest being built. Our nest at Grassy Point was getting heavier every year. By its twelfth year, the supporting branches were bending under the burden. To compensate for the tilting nest, the eagles added branches to the lower side to level it. They did the same for the next two years until the supporting branches were bent so much, the nest slipped right out of the tree. This happened in early January 2004 and by March the eagles had rebuilt a new nest in the same place and went on to fledge another eaglet, almost without a blink.

The new eagles at Trimbles' Corner displayed the same speed of nest building. In the fall of 2005 there was nothing in the tree, and by the early spring of 2006 there was a completed nest. And to think, these young eagles had probably never built a nest before.

Source of the Branches

I had assumed that eagles got their branches from the ground or from the beach. Then one day I heard a snap above and saw an eagle flying with a branch in its talons. It had broken a dead branch from a standing tree. Other people had seen similar things. Jim McLeod saw an eagle snap a branch off a tree, so he sat down to watch. The eagle came back, flew directly at a branch and snapped it off. It came back again and again. This occurred at least a dozen times in the next hour. The eagle was harvesting branches from this one tree, sufficiently rotted that the branches broke off without undue effort.

When presenting this information to a group of "eagle people," one of them confirmed that this had been her experience also. Going one step further, I mentioned never having seen an eagle take a branch off the ground. None of the others had seen this happen either. So it seems

House building.
Photo: Harry Johnson

likely that a great number of the branches used in nest building are broken from standing trees, and perhaps only a few come from the ground.

Nests are usually built in older, open-limbed trees so eaglets can excercise their six-foot wings.

Changing Nests

Eagles often leave their old nests to build new ones. Sometimes nests are poorly built and fall out of the tree. The eagle family two miles south of us, the Dysfunctional family, had a chronic problem of nests falling out of the tree. They lost four nests in eight years, losing several chicks in the process. They seemed to lack the engineering skills for proper nest building.

Then there is the Nomad family, immediately south of us. In a five-year period they lived in five different nests. They started out with one of the largest nests on Hornby Island — the result of forty or fifty years of nest building. Because eagles in the wild are not known to live for more than 30 years, this nest had to be the result of several families building over several generations. This nest finally fell out of the tree from sheer weight. They rebuilt in a tree near the beach. The next year they rebuilt inland. The following year they went back to the original tree and did the strangest of things — they built a nest twenty feet out on a branch, like a robin might do. Eagles just don't do that; they always build right next to the trunk. Needless to say, that nest fell off the branch and they moved to an old snag (dead tree) on the beach, with only two broken branches at the top where they built a nest. It makes me nervous just to look at it. All in all, they lived in five different nests in five years, and the amazing thing is they fledged an eaglet in each of the five nests.

The Dysfunctional family and the Nomad family are extreme examples of short-term housing — changing nests every year or two. At the other extreme, the Grassy Point eagles have continuously nested in the same tree for seventeen years running, now in their eighteenth year. Following, is a chart of the eagles that have nested in the same locations for longer periods than normal:

Long-term Housing

#10 Grassy Point	17 years
#21 Whaling Station Bay	11 years
#22 Helliwell Junction	10 years
#2 Bradsdadsland	7 years
#27 John and Bonita's	7 years
#9 West Carmichael	6 years

I made a study of fourteen eagle families on Hornby Island over a six-year period to see what the normal time of occupancy might be. I found that half of these families had moved one or more times during this six-year period. They are shifty creatures, I thought, and wondered how they would compare with humans. So I phoned up twenty-eight married couples on Hornby Island and asked whether they had moved in the last six years. Just like the eagles, half of them had moved one or more times in that same period. Absolutely no difference. The eagles change accommodations no more than we do.

Just as it has been unusual for the Grassy Point eagles to live in the same nest for seventeen years, I suppose it is equally unusual for my wife and I to have lived in our house for seventeen years. And very unusual, indeed, that we both happen to live right next door to each other — a happy coincidence, most convenient for this study.

Sometimes, No Apparent Reason for Changing Nests

As mentioned earlier, eagles build new nests when the old ones fall out of the tree. Far more often, they build new nests for no apparent reason at all, at least, not apparent to us. Elaine Savoie's eagles, for example, had a perfectly good nest, #6, then moved to #7 just sixty feet away. There seemed to be no advantage to the move. The new nest was the same size, the same height and the same distance from the sea. So why move? A year later, the Euston Road eagles did the same thing. They moved from nest #29 to #30, also just sixty feet away. And it is the same with many other eagles. The most common reason for moving is "no apparent reason."

People have suggested that these nests may have been infested with insect pests. This could well be the case. In a way, an eagle's nest is like an archaeological site. Digging down, there are bones, feathers, scraps of dry and rotting food and sometimes the remains of last year's chicks that didn't survive — a great environment for maggots, flies or whatever. The eagles' method of garbage disposal is to cover it all up with new twigs, branches and grass. Out of sight, out of mind.

In the case of both nests described above, the original nests remained intact for about three years and then disappeared quite quickly. They could have been recycled. That is, the sticks from the old nests may have been carried to the new nests. The old nests would certainly by a ready source of branches, and the distance of transportation most convenient. I didn't observe this actually happening, but something similar had been reported to me in another situation. I was told that eagles were methodically taking branches from an abandoned nest at the north end of Hornby Island, presumably for use in a new nest. Who knows?

A Shady Rest

I have noticed that our nest at Grassy Point is located on the side of the tree trunk shaded from the noonday sun. More accurately, it is oriented to provide shade between one and three o'clock, when it is even hotter than at noon. The chicks are the ones who would benefit mostly; they cannot fly elsewhere for shade, but are stuck in the nest throughout the summer. This might be one of the considerations eagles take into account when building nests. I'll leave it for others to check this out. Perhaps it is just a random occurrence.

Eagles Feeding

Searching for Food

Eagles spend 90 percent of their time searching for food. They do it in the most efficient way possible, by doing nothing, just perching in a tree, looking up and down the beach and out to

sea. Only when food is spotted do they fly to investigate. No energy is wasted.

Vultures, in contrast, fly along the beaches and over the fields for hours on end. They have mastered the art of soaring, covering the whole island in progressive circles, seldom

No energy is wasted.

flapping their wings. Their flight is so efficient; they expend little more energy than do the eagles while sitting on their perches. Eagles, being heavier and less skilled at soaring, stick to their own technique — perching and scanning the beach.

These two techniques of seeking food may help explain why the eagles are so territorial when vultures are not. While the eagles' food supply comes from within the range of their vision, the vultures' food supply comes from within the range of their flight (a much longer distance). Eagles then, having this limited area of food supply, are less willing to share it with others and thus are far more territorial, certainly with other eagles.

Because the food supply of eagles is so dependent on vision, it is not surprising that their eyesight is so good — equivalent to looking through ten-power binoculars. And this is supplemented by a few cunning tricks, such as those used by the Polynesians when navigating the oceans. By steering towards clouds, the Polynesians were sure to find an island beneath. In a similar manner, eagles, spotting circling vultures, might find food beneath. And the presence of gulls offshore might signal a school of herring.

One way or another, eagles are highly dependent on their vision for survival and indeed, their eyesight lives up to their "eagle-eye" reputation.

Methods of Retrieving Food

Once they spot food, eagles usually take it "on the fly," like an aerial fast food restaurant. They fly low over their food target, snatch it up with their talons and keep flying to a rock or perch for feeding. Most people have seen this on TV nature programs, showing an eagle snapping a fish from the water. This method of retrieving food applies equally to fish in the water or to birds, chickens, opossums, or mink on the land.

A friend saw an eagle catch a mallard and tumble into the water with it. The eagle tried several times to lift it out of the water but failed. It let go of the mallard, circled around and flew back full speed to successfully snatch the duck out of the water. In full flight, eagles have more momentum than when attempting to lift directly from the water or directly from the land.

But even this "fly-by and snatch" method has its limits. If the prey is too large, the eagle has no choice other than to swim it to shore; and if it is on land the eagle has no choice but to consume it where it is found.

When I first began studying eagles I threw a two-pound fish on the beach so I could take pictures of the eagle eating, but the eagle snapped up the fish before I could get a single picture. Now I know if I want to have the eagle stop and feed, I would have to throw out an eight-pound salmon, too heavy to carry away. And if I had an eight-pound salmon, I would eat it myself (8 lb x $9/lb = $72). I heard of one person who, upon seeing an eagle swimming to shore with a salmon, rushed down to the beach and took the salmon for himself. Very mean. Such a person cannot be a member of my eagle club.

Catching Fish

Bald eagles are thought of as being "fish eagles." For Hornby Island eagles, this description is more in the sense of "fish-eating" rather than "fish-catching." When they fly or swim in with a salmon, I suspect they have retrieved one that is injured or dying, and have not actually caught a salmon.

Our female eagle on the beach with a dogfish. *Photos: Afona Peters*

I have actually seen our eagles catch live healthy salmon, but in unusual circumstances. It has occurred only on extreme high tides in November and December. They perch in trees leaning over the beach and peer down into two or three feet of clear winter water. Upon spotting a salmon, they drop straight down, talons first, completely immersed, and come up with the fish, much in the fashion of an osprey. These salmon were not large ones, only twelve to fourteen inches long, but sufficiently nourishing to keep them going for a few more days.

Specific Foods

Salmon

Salmon is by far the most important food for eagles, not so much because of the few they catch from the sea, but more in relation to the millions of carcasses left along the rivers every fall after the salmon have spawned.

The Columbia River, flowing into the Pacific Ocean between Washington State and Oregon, had tremendous runs of salmon, but 100 dams later the number of salmon has declined. The Fraser River, draining into the Georgia Strait near Vancouver, is now the world's most productive salmon river. The miracle is that neither the Fraser River nor its main tributary, the Thompson, has a single dam blocking the passage of fish. In 1913, 100,000,000 salmon ran up the Fraser each fall and even today 30,000,000 still make the trip.

Most spectacular of all is the Adams River run of sockeye salmon. Although the Adams River is only fifty feet wide and two feet deep, it is spellbinding to watch 5,000,000 salmon swim by in a two- or three-week period of time. You can almost walk across the river on their backs.

This may be the most dramatic salmon run of them all, but

the same thing is happening all along the coast of British Columbia. There are hundreds of rivers and streams around the Georgia Strait, and hundreds more along the coast to Alaska. Each has its own run of salmon, sometimes several species and occasionally all five species. Every fall these salmon swim up the rivers and tributaries as far as they can go, lay their eggs, and die soon after, leaving thousands of carcasses — a mass of food for crows, gulls, eagles, bears, wolves and other creatures. Even the forests benefit from the resulting excrement spread by the birds and animals. When examining the annual rings of trees, the wide rings, representing rapid growth, coincide with the years of outstanding salmon runs.

Eagle feeding on salmon at Brackendale.
Photo: Roy Hamaguchi

By mid-August, the fledged eaglets are strong enough to begin the migration north to the salmon rivers. I had assumed the parents flew with their eaglets, showing them the way, but have been informed otherwise. The eaglets make the trip entirely on their own — by instinct. There are numerous salmon rivers in the north for the eaglets to fly to as they learn to forage for themselves. The best known is at Haines, Alaska "the World's Largest Concentration of Bald Eagles," 700 miles north of Hornby Island. The spawning starts there early and the eagles accumulate, with their numbers peaking in mid-November. The eagles work their way south until reaching Brackendale, near Vancouver, "The Eagle Capital of the World." They arrive in December and peak early in January. Many of the eagles seen at Haines, Alaska, will be the same ones seen later at Brackendale, doing the circuit, from north to south.

We can follow some of the eagles to their next food supply, the Boundary Bay Landfill, near Vancouver. John Elliott and other biologists for Environment Canada found that the eagle numbers peaked there on February 26, after the salmon runs at Brackendale were finished.

After the salmon runs at Brackendale, on to the Vancouver garbage dump.

Going one step further, the migrating eagles seem to carry on to Hornby Island for the herring spawn that occurs early every March. At that time we often have an invasion of 400 to 600 eagles. Are these the same eagles completing the food circuit? And then after Hornby, where do they go? There is a lot to learn yet about eagle migrations.

I will be discussing a variety of foods used by the eagles but not one of them has the importance of salmon. This is the food — available in great quantities from September to January — that nourishes the newly fledged eaglets through their first winter. And the same applies to their second, third and fourth years on the migration circuits. But even this massive food supply is not always dependable. In the winter of 2006/07, for example, the extreme rainfall at Brackendale washed all the carcasses down the river to the sea. When I visited in mid-January (the peak time), I saw only three eagles — not quite the Eagle Capital of the World. Nevertheless, most rivers are reliable in most years. Salmon is still number one.

Herring

Like salmon, the herring are also an important source of nutrition. The salmon help the eagles through the winter and the herring are the fuel energizing the spring breeding season.

Herring are fish from six to nine inches long that swim closely packed in large schools, which may be up to a mile long, a quarter mile wide and 200 feet deep. Each spring the herring migrate from the Pacific Ocean into the Georgia Strait. It is estimated that in most years their total biomass is around 100,000 tons. Considering that a typical gravel truck can carry ten tons, these herring would fill 10,000 such trucks — a lot of food.

Several hundred herring skiffs fish herring for their eggs, a gourmet food in Japan. *Photo: Peter Brady*

In early March the female herring come close to shore and attach their eggs to the seaweed, and the males fill the water with milt, thus fertilizing the eggs, and noticeably changing the colour of the water in the process.

In the weeks before the spawn, birds of all kinds congregate in anticipation of the great feast to come, as do the seals and sea lions. Some 400 or more wandering eagles arrive at Hornby, many of them immatures (speckled brown). They perch in trees along the shore, sometimes five or six per tree, unchallenged by the local eagles. There is food for everyone.

Two or three weeks in advance of the spawn, the schools of herring come closer to the shore. Masses of gulls can be seen above the herring, mapping their presence in the sea below. The active forces at work are the murres, loons, cormorants, and mergansers diving down to feed, frightening the herring to the surface where the gulls snap them up.

Watching for herring.

Eagles fly out to the schools of herring, slashing their talons into the water, snapping up two or three herring per talon. The immature eagles, however, are so foolish. An immature eagle no sooner catches a herring than two others attack it. In the ensuing struggle, the herring drops in the water and escapes. If one of the attacking eagles does succeed in stealing a herring, it becomes the new target and loses again. This happens over and over. Rarely do any of them succeed. So much energy expended for such meagre results. Immature behaviour, indeed!

After watching this, I am soon talking to myself. If only each eagle minded its own business and caught its own herring, there would be enough for them all. If more civilized, they would have the rule "don't steal," and they would all be better off. On further reflection, however, there may be a higher wisdom behind this behaviour. It may be toughening them up for the day a real food shortage occurs. The tough ones, well practiced in theft, will be the ones to survive.

As the day of spawning approaches, the sky is criss-crossed with birds, the beaches are white with gulls and the sea is alive with ducks. There is excitement in the air, and a chorus of bird cries intermingles with the barking of sea lions, reminiscent of the once popular recording, "Ebb Tide." Coming at the end of a long and hungry winter, the herring spawn is truly the beginning of spring — a time of rejoicing.

Pale blue water and foam mark the beginning of the herring spawn.
Photo: Peter Brady

The spawn starts in the morning. We wake up to an intensified excitement and there it is, the first spawn. The sea is changing colour in front of our eyes, from a deep blue to a pale cloudy turquoise, like glacial water in a mountain lake. This cloudy water starts at Grassy Point, to our left, slowly moves in front of our house, then into the bay and around Sandstone Point. An hour later it gets to Tralee Point, a mile south of us. This has opened up a new source of food, not just the herring themselves, but now the eggs as well. Many of the eggs do not get attached to the seaweed and are floating freely in the water. The smaller gulls and ducks are devouring these. The crows, too, are down at the shoreline gobbling up the eggs and sometimes hooking a herring from the shallow water.

Herring for everybody. *Photo: Donna Baker*

The concentration of birds is now at its peak. All the larger loons, gulls, cormorants and fish-eating ducks have followed the herring to this narrow band along the beach and are now intermingled with the smaller gulls, ducks, and crows feeding on the eggs. The herons are also there, wading in a foot of water, spearing herring to their heart's content.

This feeding frenzy goes on for a week or more. The herring spawn is a miraculous thing, a kick-start to the breeding season just around the corner. All the creatures are fattening up for the year to come. The eagles lay their eggs just two weeks after the spawn.

Odds and Ends Related to Herring

Herring Eggs, the Food of Kings It is common to see two or three inches of herring eggs washed up along the shore. One year I tried eating them. All the birds just love them. The Japanese pay a fortune for herring roe, and other people call fish eggs "caviar," the food of kings. Accordingly, I put the herring eggs in the frying pan and turned them into a sticky rubbery mass like tapioca, without flavour. Horrible! Perhaps it's the way you prepare them, or the spices you use; maybe they are better raw. I must try again next year.

Herring Eggs as a Fertilizer One year I took several wheelbarrow loads of herring eggs from the beach for garden fertilizer, putting it in a pile to decompose. People who know about herring eggs will be holding their noses; herring eggs become revolting. So, I covered them over with four inches of garden soil. A month or two later some friends visited us with their little dog, Ringo. He dug into the pile, now a squishy quagmire, and rolled over in it, as any good dog would do. They never brought Ringo back to our house.

The First Full Moon of March Many people believe the herring spawn happens on the first full moon of March. I've always believed this full moon stuff is a myth, but checked it out anyway. I made a chart showing the dates of the first herring spawn over the past twelve years. I then looked up the dates of the first full moon in March over this same period, and marked them on the chart. There is absolutely no correlation between herring spawning and the full moon.

I then phoned the Department of Fisheries and Oceans (DFO) at Nanaimo and got a similar opinion. One biologist, now retired, had also tried to relate full moon tides to herring spawning and likewise had found no relationship. What they do believe, however, is that the time of spawning is determined by a combination of water temperature (8°C/46.4°F) and the amount of light available. A period of clear weather might speed up the process, and cloudy weather might slow it down.

Midshipmen

Where salmon carcasses sustain the eagles through winter and herring re-energize them in spring, a lesser-known fish, the midshipman, is the main food of summer. The midshipman grows up to nine inches long. It has a fairly large head tapering to its tail, rather like a sculpin or bullhead, but with no noticeable spines or scales. They are found in tidal pools at low tide, hidden under seaweed or beneath large rocks, and hence are not easily seen.

In late spring, the midshipmen migrate from the Pacific Ocean to beaches along the west coast. The males seek suitable nesting places among the rocks and begin singing — a humming sound, like a miniature chainsaw. For this reason, they are sometimes called the "singing" fish. The singing does two things: it warns off other males and attracts females. If attracted by the singing, females lay their eggs and leave — nothing else. The males fertilize the eggs, guard them until they hatch and protect the young fish until well into August.

My neighbour, Gordie, and I were down on the beach at low tide looking for midshipmen. He wondered how they got

Long, gradually sloping beaches, loaded with rocks and tidal pools, are ideal for midshipmen. Crows and eagles feed there constantly at low tides.

that name. I had read that they are supposed to have two rows of buttons, like a naval officer. Gordie immediately picked up a midshipman and turned it over. There they were, the two rows of buttons, on its underside. I had never seen them before, because I had been too squeamish to lift one up — and still am.

A biologist in Washington State was visiting a beach to listen for singing fish. The police had just checked a graduation party nearby, confiscated liquor and marijuana, and then spotted him. He looked suspicious, so they asked him what he was doing. "Listening for singing fish," he explained.

There is a special relationship between eagles and crows, and it's related to the midshipmen. People often observe crows harassing an eagle while it sits minding its own business. One after another the crows dive-bomb the eagle's head, forcing it to duck or lash out in self-defence; this goes on relentlessly. Observers feel sorry for the eagles and wonder why the crows are so mean. But it is the eagles that are mean; they steal the crows' food, and the crows are just retaliating.

Starting in spring, crows work the beaches, hunting for food. At low tide, they check the tidal pools, look under seaweed and turn over pebbles; churning up shrimp, sculpins, eel-like fish called blennies, midshipmen and other edibles — all under the watchful eye of the eagle. The moment the crows find something, the eagle swoops down and takes it. Smaller things, like shrimp, can be gobbled down before the eagle arrives but not so with midshipmen, the largest of the tidal pool creatures.

Eagles are constantly stealing midshipmen from crows. On one occasion I saw an eagle swoop down and take a midshipman from the crows while a squadron of furious crows pursued it, buzzing it from every direction. The eagle landed on "dinner rock" (a favourite eating place) and consumed the midshipman. By the time it had finished, the crows had found a second midshipman. The eagle took that one also. This goes on day after day, all summer long, eagles stealing the crows' food and crows harassing the eagles. You can understand how the crows must feel.

At first, I thought the midshipmen were an incidental food, but now feel it is the main food of summer, especially for the nourishment of eagle chicks. The midshipmen arrive on our beaches in early May, coinciding exactly with the hatching of the first eagle chicks. They are available in great numbers throughout the summer until mid-August, also coinciding with the time the eaglets are developing until their migration. It is hard to imagine a better match of supply with demand, especially in the provision of food for the new offspring. As a result, I looked upon the midshipmen as a "baby" food. However, in the last two years, when neither eggs nor chicks survived, the eagles were taking midshipmen from the crows as much as ever, but eating them themselves. So the midshipmen are food for everyone. Presumably the crows get to keep a few themselves.

One other thing, the conflict between the eagles and crows is not outright warfare but simply a conflict over food, lasting only while the midshipmen are here. The rest of the year is peaceful. The crows have forgiven the crimes of summer and get on with their lives. That is, until the midshipmen return the following May and the battles begin once again.

The Shrimp Fishery

The shrimp fishery provides another source of food for eagles. Shrimp fishing is done by dragging nets along the bottom or near the bottom. The shrimp are the "target" catch and the fish taken by accident are the "bycatch." The accidental catch includes hake, sole, rockfish, lingcod, dogfish, and many smaller and unusual creatures. To limit the amount of bycatch, the shrimp nets are equipped with "bycatch excluders," which are special exits that allow swimming fish to escape before the nets are drawn in. But the system is not 100 percent effective, judging by the number of gulls following each shrimp boat.

The gulls pick off the small stuff, whereas the eagles are only interested in the larger fish like hake and rockfish. When these fish are brought to the surface, their air bladders expand like a balloon, so they are unable to swim back down and they become easy pickings for the eagles. I used to think the shrimp fishery was wasteful, but from the eagles' point of view, it isn't.

Stolen Food

We have already discussed eagles stealing fish from ospreys, and stealing midshipmen from crows, but that is just the beginning. Wherever there is food, eagles will attempt to steal it. The sloppy eating habits of sea lions provide the eagles another opportunity for such behaviour. Sea lions, common around Hornby Island in winter, are like seals but much larger. Being fussy eaters, they bite the fleshy belly out of a fish and leave the rest. Both gulls and eagles compete furiously for the leftovers. The first eagle on location snatches the remains from the sea lion's mouth, almost before it has completed its bite.

Eagles attempt to do the same thing with otters but rarely succeed — otters are too quick and cunning. A group of eight otters came swimming along the beach chasing fish. They are so active — up to the surface for thirty seconds, and then back under again. Each time an otter surfaces, it has a fish in its mouth, gobbles it down and dives under again. I had no idea there were so many fish around. Our eagle flew down on the otters, trying to steal a fish, but the moment it was in striking range, the otters dove under. The eagle tried it over and over but never succeeded — nor did it slow up the otters' fishing.

While this was going on, a heron was doing something similar. The heron was flying from one rock to another, following the otters as they progressed along the shore. It was hoping to spear a desperate fish swimming to the shallows to escape the otters, but it never succeeded either.

Another sea lion story was just related to me. Andrea, at Ford Cove, heard a great commotion during the past herring spawn — the barking of sea lions and the screeching of eagles. The sea lions, in a concerted effort, were herding the herring against the sandstone shelves along the shoreline, so they could gobble them down in great concentrations. In desperation, the herring were jumping out of the water onto the sandstone shelves, only to be devoured by the dozens of waiting eagles.

A most unusual situation occurred related to dunlins, a falcon and our eagles. Dunlins are small shore birds that fly in large flocks and in extremely tight formations. You wonder how they avoid having collisions with each other. Especially amazing is the way they suddenly change directions, at one time appearing black and in the next instant white, depending on whether their under sides are showing or their top sides. At the moment of direction change, every individual dunlin moves at the same instant and in the same direction. It's not like a flock of geese following the leader or like a swarm of bees. How do they know precisely when to change directions, and more amazing, how do they know which way to go? These sudden and frequent direction changes are there to baffle predators such as falcons.

Despite this, I saw a falcon dive into a flock of dunlins, knocking one of them tumbling into the sea. At that moment, our eagle swooped down from its perch and snatched the dunlin from the sea before the falcon had time to retrieve it. Typical eagle behaviour.

Another situation relates to a gull and a large crab. A gull, perhaps George or Alice, was diving into the water attempting to get something. It is rare for a glaucus-winged gull to dive right under like a duck. After three of four tries, it came up with a large eating crab, legs and pincers clawing as crabs do, a bit unnerving even for the gull. It tore off one leg, began eating it and then abruptly flew away. You guessed it — the eagle! It landed and ate the crab at leisure.

Benjamin Franklin, signatory of the Declaration of Independence and of the Constitution of the United States, knew all about the behaviour of the bald eagle and didn't think it was appropriate as a symbol for the United States of America:

> He is a Bird of bad moral Character. He does not get his Living honestly. You may see him perched on some dead Tree near the River, where, too lazy to fish for himself, he watches the Labour of the Fishing Hawk (Osprey), and when that diligent Bird has at length taken a Fish … The Bald Eagle pursues him and takes it from him.

Incidentally, look how Benjamin Franklin was spelling "labour" — the English and Canadian way rather than "labor," the American spelling. The change must have occurred since that time.

Carrion

Carrion (dead animals) is the main food of vultures, and a significant source of food for eagles. Most important in this category are (1) deer; (2) seals; (3) sea lions.

Deer When walking my dog at night, I feel quite pleased that there are no bears, cougars or wolves on Hornby Island, unlike most of the rest of British Columbia. As a result, we have an over-population of deer, which causes an over-browsing of leaves, berries and shrubs, and worst of all, an over-browsing of my garden. By the end of most winters, a number of deer have died off, mainly the young ones, becoming food for the eagles. Also, a number of deer are killed on the roads. The highway crews transport these carcasses to the gravel pit, again for the eagles.

Seals I often count 150 to 200 seals basking on Flora Island, just off Hornby Island, and there are many more. Each summer (birthing season) people find newly born seals along the shoreline, many in good health, some abandoned and some dead — more food for the eagles and vultures. At any time in the year, a few adult seals die off from old age, or whatever.

Sea Lions Sea lions are here in great numbers all winter. When not feeding, they sleep in groups, called "rafts," usually with one flipper up in the air and their heads under water. By automatic reflex, their heads come up every two minutes or so for a breath and go under again, all while fast asleep. One November, I counted 2,000 sea lions sleeping in one giant raft.

The sea lions visiting Hornby for the winter are all males, some of them weighing 2,000 pounds, the size of a small car. The females stay at their breeding grounds, some off the coast of California and some up north. The males come here for our fish and herring, gaining 400 pounds in weight and then burning it up again at the breeding grounds in spring, fighting over females.

Again, a number of these die off each year, much to the dread of waterfront property owners. Two thousand pounds of rotting flesh — a revolting smell! The total mass is far more than the eagles and vultures can consume.

Carrion is shared between the vultures and eagles in the summer, but is exclusively for the eagles throughout the winter when the vultures are in California and Mexico. The ravens also get their portion throughout the year.

Small Mammals

Another possible source of food is small mammals, but this is rare. A neighbour saw an eagle pierce its talons into the back of a mink, which immediately turned into a writhing, screeching, biting, bundle of energy. The eagle flew the length of the beach and back, clutching the mink, but not knowing what to do with it. It landed on a log and the two of them toppled to the beach. The eagle tore some fur off the mink and the mink retaliated with a slashing bite at the eagle's neck, and made its escape.

Small opossums could possibly be another food for eagles. A few opossum carcasses appear in eagles' nests, but they are most likely road-kill. It seems that mink, opossums and other small mammals are of little significance in the diet of eagles.

The Myth of Cats

However, stories keep coming up about cats. A long time ago, an Internet story told of fifteen cat collars being found in an eagle's nest. That same story has come to me many times since, always with the same number of collars. I checked the Internet recently and found a massive increase in such events. One site told of finding a nest, not just full of cat collars but also dog collars. Another site told of an outdoor guide on the west coast of Vancouver Island telling the starry-eyed listeners about forty-two cat collars being found in a nest at Victoria. People on tours just love such stories. And not to be outdone, a story from Massachusetts tells of students finding an active eagle's nest, tearing it apart and finding sixty cat collars.

This last story came from an elementary school student — perhaps a creative writing class. It's great to see young people being so interested in eagles. But it also shows the tendency of all people, young or old, to be captivated by bizarre events and prone to repeat them. The psychology of rumours and myths must be a fascinating study. Why do some concepts take a hold and persist? There are a number of myths associated with eagles that just won't go away. And as you have already guessed, I feel that the cat collar stories are one of these myths.

First, in eighteen years of eagle watching I have seen no cat bones in an eagle's nest or beneath it, nor have I heard anyone who has.

Second, there is the matter of what weight an eagle can lift off the ground. I know that an eagle can easily fly with a widgeon (just under two pounds) and can fly with a mallard (just under three pounds). I have seen them swimming to shore with four or five pound salmon — meaning they were too heavy to lift out of the water. From things like this, I feel that eagles could probably lift six pounds for a short run, but a maximum of four pounds, with difficulty, up to nest height. That would eliminate the likelihood of many cats ending up in an eagle's nest.

Third, think of the fighting angle. If a two-pound mink can challenge an eagle, what damage could an eight-pound cat do? Cats are no pushovers.

Fourth, if forty-two collars were found, what happened to the forty-two skulls? Eagles don't eat skulls. The nest would be overflowing with skulls and the ground below also. No mention is ever made of the skulls, just of the collars. Truth is not an essential element of a myth. Anyway, you can be assured that cats are not a significant part of an eagle's diet, or for that matter, are small mammals of any kind.

Summarizing the Topic of Food

We have now discussed salmon, herring, midshipmen, the shrimp fishery, stolen food, carrion, mammals, and cats. In closing, I should mention ducks and gulls. In the summer, eagles rarely catch these birds, but winter takes its toll, especially on the old, injured and sickly birds. The more severe the winter, the greater the die-off and the more food there is for the eagles. Even then, these scrawny carcasses are lean pickings, but hungry eagles can't be choosy.

That leaves the garbage dumps, always a fallback for eagles. The nearest one is forty miles away, but even then not out of range — just a one-hour flight at cruising speed. And as a last resort, there are the neighbours' chickens. The survival of eagles is greatly assisted by the variety of foods they consume.

Collapse of the Salmon

The most drastic environmental change in the last few years has been the collapse of the Coho salmon stocks in the Georgia Strait (See graph A). Each year, the coho salmon would come from the Pacific to feed in the Georgia Strait for the summer. After fattening up, they ran up the local rivers in October for spawning. The coho salmon were the main fish for sports fishing; they lived near the surface, were great fighters, and were around in the summer, the most pleasant time to be out in a small boat. An average of 180,000 coho were caught each year in the Georgia Strait up to the crash of 1994, and hardly a fish has been caught since. There has been no

(A)   COHO SALMON CAUGHT BY SPORT FISHERMEN
IN THE GEORGIA STRAIT

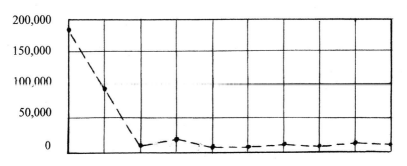

recovery. Strangely enough, the same numbers of coho still spawn up the local rivers in October. Instead of spending the summer feeding in the Georgia Strait, the coho salmon now feed on the west coast of Vancouver Island and make a dash for their spawning rivers in October, few being caught en route. Why this has happened seems to be a mystery, but it is interesting to speculate on the effect of this drastic change on killer whales and on eagles.

Effect on Whales

There are a number of different groups of killer whales, each having a special diet and each tending to restrict itself to that particular food. Like the eagles, the resident killer whales of the Georgia Strait are also salmon eaters. Although they occasionally eat rockfish, hake and herring, they never eat alternative foods available, such as ducks, seals, sea lions or larger whales. On the other hand, the transient killer whales passing through these same waters, are almost exactly the opposite — they eat seals, sea lions and porpoise, but seldom salmon. The killer whales of Norway feed on herring. And the once thriving killer whales of Eden, Australia fed exclusively on humpback whales; but when the humpbacks were hunted to

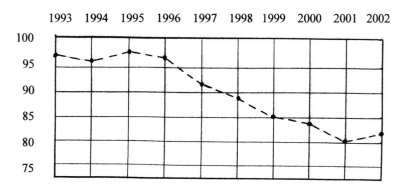

(B)   POPULATION OF SOUTHERN KILLER WHALES

near extinction in the 1930s, the killer whales of Eden died off soon after. In conclusion, killer whales seem to specialize in their food preferences and are slow to make adjustments. Putting all your eggs in one basket is a risky habit. It is possible that the drop in killer whale population in the Georgia Strait is related to the crash of the salmon stock (Graph B). Note: there has been a similar decline in the chinook salmon stock, another important food of the killer whales.

Effect on Eagles

With the crash of the salmon, people on Hornby Island were concerned for the eagles. What would they feed on? Soon after the crash, the eagles began raiding the heron colony at Tralee Point. It is difficult to assess whether this would have happened anyway because of the increasing eagle population, or whether it was a direct response to the loss of salmon. Whatever the case, by the year 2000 there had also been an extreme drop in the heron population (caused by the eagles). Despite the loss of both salmon and young herons to eat, the eagles went on to fledge more eaglets than ever in the years 2001 and 2002 (Graph C). The varied diet of the eagles probably places them in a better position for survival than the whales with their more restrictive diets.

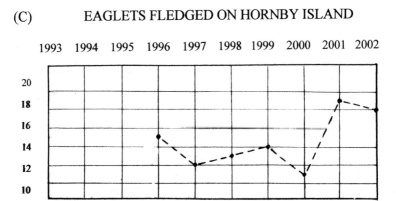

(C)   EAGLETS FLEDGED ON HORNBY ISLAND

Eagle Reproduction

Saint Valentine's Day and Eagles

One of the oldest beliefs has been that birds choose their mates on Saint Valentine's Day, February 14. The eagles of Hornby Island follow this dictate. In actual fact, the eagles mate on that date…and in the two weeks before Saint Valentine's…and in the two weeks after. In other words, eagles mate throughout the month of February. But they stretch things a little more, to include the last few days of January and well into March, but at no other time of the year. All in all, one could consider that eagles mate in February, the month of Saint Valentine.

And where do they mate? Rarely, if ever, in their nest. Behind our house is the "Love Tree." I first witnessed the eagles mating there and named the tree accordingly, but they have seldom used it since, even for perching on. Nonetheless, the name has stuck. Generally they use one of their other perch trees.

And here is how mating actually occurs. You will see two eagles (in February) sitting side by side on a branch. Watch them edge closer to each other. At this point you would expect gentle whisperings, but instead there is extremely loud chatter, as if they were a mile apart. The male hops on the back of the female, wings out for balance, and five seconds later hops off again. That is it. Well not quite. The same thing will occur several times in any one season. I used to break this mating into two categories, "procreational" mating and "recreational" mating, the former being the serious stuff to have chicks, but really I can't distinguish which is which. Perhaps a topic for a PhD?

Many readers have heard a romantic version of eagle mating, which I do not believe, but will repeat for the sake of Saint Valentine. It begins high in the skies. The eagles hold each other's talons and begin a long spiralling free fall, head over heals, down and down, finally separating before reaching the ground. One version compares this to a renewal of marital vows. Walt Whitman wrote a poem about this called, "The Dalliance of the Eagles":

> The rushing amorous contact high in space together,
> The clinching interlocking claws, a living, fierce, gyrating wheel,
> Four beating wings, beaks, a swirling mass tight grappling,
> In turning tumbling clustering loops, strait downward falling

From time to time, eagles do soar high in the sky and occasionally tumble down with talons grasped, but I question Walt Whitman's interpretation of this event. I think he was reading something into it that was not there, that it represents a fevered state of mind more than reality. In such a state, I'm sure he could watch a grove of trees blowing in the wind, and see branches entwined in fond embraces, rubbing against each other, and produce another masterpiece, "The Dalliance of the Oak Trees," leaving people enthralled for generations to come.

I will present another explanation for the talon-grasping behaviour. The young of most species practice combat in the form of play fighting, such as the mock-battles of puppies and the wrestling of bear cubs. "Play" is essential practice for the struggles of later years. Why wouldn't young eagles do the same? How do they become such proficient fighters without earlier practice? And how would Walt Whitman know it was an amorous contact? How would he know the tumbling eagles were male and female? It is difficult to tell the difference even up close.

The real version of nature is sufficiently impressive for me. Anyone who saw the Hornby Island Eagles on the webcam knows they are totally devoted to each other. Through rain and storms they kept their eggs dry. Despite failed eggs and buffeting by more recent winter storms, they are still together. Over the past seventeen years they've done lots of mating, but never once have I seen them having a "dalliance." There is no need for poetic fantasies such as presented by Walt Whitman.

Productivity of the Grassy Point Eagles

The Grassy Point eagles have fledged fifteen eaglets over a seventeen-year period, just under one eaglet per year. This is considered average productivity for this area of British Columbia. Further south, the productivity is higher, and further north it is lower.

In the years when no eaglets were fledged, people have wondered if it was because no eggs were laid. But eggs were laid in every year. Starting in the last week in March, when eggs are normally laid, the two eagles began taking shifts in and out of the nest, signifying there is at least one egg in the nest to be incubated. Eggs were laid even in the years no eaglets were fledged. In many of these same years, starting on May 1 when eggs normally hatch, the eagles began bringing fish to the nest, signifying there is at least one chick in the nest needing food. My conclusion is that failure to fledge eaglets is rarely because of failure to lay eggs, but because the eggs failed to hatch or the chicks failed to survive.

Year	No. Fledged	Year	No. Fledged	Year	No. Fledged
1990	1	1996	1	2002	0
1991	1	1997	1	2003	2
1992	2	1998	2	2004	1
1993	1	1999	0	2005	0
1994	2	2000	1	2006	0
1995	0	2001	0		
				Total:	**15**

In 2005 when I first had a video camera on the nest, two eggs were laid. The first egg hatched, but six days later, the chick died. The chick in the second egg pecked a hole in the egg and could be heard peeping, but died while still inside its shell. The following year, when millions were watching the eagles, neither egg hatched, nor did the chicks even start to peck a hole in their shells.

Age might have been a factor in the fledging failures of more recent years. Looking at the table to the left, you can see that in the first five years, seven eaglets were fledged, while in the last five years only three were fledged. Eagles may become less productive as they get older.

At that time they were twenty-three years of age. This calculation is based on six years to mature plus seventeen years of nesting. Considering that the oldest recorded age for an eagle in the wild is thirty years, these two eagles are well past "middle-age." So I'm resigned to the fact that my next few years will be spent observing eagles in their old age.

A friend informed me about two eagles in a Winnipeg zoo. They were forty years of age when they laid an egg. Even more amazing, they went on to successfully fledge an eaglet. Mind you, living in the wild is much more difficult than living in a zoo. It does illustrate, however, that further reproduction by our eagles is not a biological impossibility. Perhaps eagles continue laying eggs until their last day? It will be interesting to follow their next few years.

Another factor may also affect productivity — food supply. Benn Kramer's eagles at Bradsdadsland were fed fresh fish every day. As a result they fledged seventeen eaglets in ten years, way above average. So I looked over the record of our eagles to relate it to food supply. The only significant change in their diet might be the drastic collapse of the Coho salmon starting in 1994 and hitting rock bottom in 1995 (see graph on page 73). Strangely enough, 1995 was the first year our eagles failed to fledge an eaglet, and their productivity has never been as high since then. Was the lack of salmon the cause?

The question remains. Is the drop in productivity because of age, because of food supply, because of other factors, or some combination of these factors? A lot more research is required before any reasonable conclusions can be made.

Stages in the Life of a Young Eagle

Four Days Before Laying an Egg The eagles on Hornby Island usually lay their eggs in the last week of March. About four days before this, the female settles down in the nest and is reluctant to leave, perhaps expecting to lay an egg at any moment. Normally, each eagle looks after its own food requirements, but at this time the male becomes most attentive, gently placing fish near her head so she doesn't have to leave the nest.

The Laying of Eggs I have an excellent video of the eagle laying an egg. The lighting is excellent, the eagle is close up and facing the camera. Her feathers bristle like a porcupine and you can see the muscular contractions pushing the egg on its way — about one contraction every three seconds. There is a distinct grunt with each contraction, and after approximately four minutes the egg is laid. A second egg is usually laid four days after the first one.

Sitting on the Eggs After laying the egg, there is a fifteen-minute period before the female sits on the egg to keep it warm. It has been suggested that this is to allow the eggshell time to harden. After a long first shift, the female steps aside for the male to take over and they alternate for thirty-five days until the egg hatches. The shifts seem to last an average of two hours each, but vary in length, sometimes lasting for five hours and at other times for just half an hour. The changeover is quick, not exposing the eggs for long, although on warmer days the eggs may be exposed for two or three minutes.

Hatching When first hatched, the new chick is incredibly small and utterly helpless. The parent looks at it as if wondering, "What is this?" But no doubt it is admiring the new member of the family. Within an hour, the new chick is able to work itself into a wobbly sit-up position. Soon after, the parent tucks the tiny chick under its body, using its great pointed talons, which seem better suited for battle than for childcare. However, there is a gentleness involved when around eggs or chicks; the eagles always roll their talons under, walking on their knuckles, so as not to harm them.

The First Feed About fifteen hours after hatching, the chick is ready for its first feed. A little head pushes itself out from under the parental feathers and squirms its way out. It's time to be fed. The parent leans forward with a morsel of fish until the chick reaches up. Then the parent pulls back and swallows it. The same thing happens two or three times more, like a form of child-abuse, but more likely to get the chick's digestive juices working. Once started, the chick keeps gobbling down its food for another twenty minutes, and then falls asleep.

Pecking the Head A month later the relationship of the chicks can be disturbing. The first hatched chick, being four days older than the second chick, has a size advantage that lasts the next two months, and it uses this advantage by pecking at the head of the smaller one without mercy. People watching the Victoria-area chicks on the webcam were often upset at their behaviour, but both chicks survived this period and went on to successfully fledge. Perhaps this sibling rivalry toughens them up for adult survival.

On to Full Size Another month later and it is yet another scene. It is almost a matter of parental survival. The sweet little chicks (who pecked each other's heads) are now the size of their parents and are called eaglets. They get aggressive when their parents arrive with food, screaming and pushing to be first. Almost fearing for their own safety, the parents will drop the food in the nest and escape. Within a half hour after feeding, an amazing transformation occurs; the eaglets change from monsters to angels — two brown balls, fast asleep.

Preparing for the First Flight I remember the "twins" preparing for their first flight in the summer of 1998. There was a stiff wind that day. The eaglets just had to extend their wings to feel an immediate uplift. With ever so slight of a jump, they rose up a foot or two in the air. This was exhilarating. They took turns, peeping with excitement. Then they jumped from one side of the nest to the other and then out to a branch and back. Sometimes their landings were awkward but, with repetition, they improved. Then they jumped up, with an additional flap or two of the wings, and found themselves six or seven feet in the air, sometimes too high for comfort. This went on, over and over. The next day they made their first flight, to the "Babysitting Tree," seventy feet away. A bit unnerved, they were reluctant to make the flight back to the nest. The parents enticed them back with food.

The First Landing The first landings made by eaglets are often disasters. Neighbours reported the first landing made by their eaglet. As the eaglet approached the branch, it was flying too fast. It grabbed at the branch but kept on rotating over the top like a gymnast, ending upside down below the branch, eventually holding on with one talon only. After a time, it flopped down through a few more branches and caught onto another branch, still upside down. With a few more manoeuvres, it finally extricated itself from the tangle. But the eaglets learn rapidly; in three weeks they are ready for a three-hundred-mile migration up the coast to the salmon streams.

Video Cameras and Web Cameras

Video Camera in the Eagle Tree

After fifteen years observing eagles from the ground, I installed a video camera above the eagle nest. This could not have happened without Bob Chappell, a retired electronic system designer from Victoria, who had put cameras in the nests of owls, ducks and other birds. These nests are lit with infrared lighting and wired for sound, resulting in wonderful videos. He also installed cameras focused on eagles at the mouth of the Goldstream River (Victoria) and cameras immersed in the river, focused on the spawning salmon, so visitors to the park can watch on screens, creating no disturbance.

Bob Chappell, the video camera expert (left), holding the camera box clad in bark.

With Bob offering to assist me, I started to get things rolling. I asked the owners of the eagle tree property if I could put a camera up their tree, and they gave permission. Then I asked permission from the Ministry of Environment. You can't meddle with eagle trees without good reason; it has to be for a scientific purpose or for education. "Well, I'm planning to write a book," I explained. "That would be education." This

Top Jed Young, standing in the eagles' nest, 120 feet above the ground, installing a back-up camera.
Middle Doug Wood, who strung the co-axial cable from the camera to our house.
Bottom The author and Jed Young with the back-up camera.

got a smile (everyone is going to write a book) and it was suggested that I should associate myself with the local colleges. I got the blessings of Malaspina University College at Nanaimo and the North Island College at Courtenay. At the same time, the Wildlife Tree Stewards (WiTS) also gave full support to the project. So, I got the OK from the Ministry of Environment.

I was now working under a deadline. It was the beginning of September. The eagles were away on migration and would be returning on the first day of October, just one month remaining. The camera had to be installed while they were away. Bob Chappell had now purchased the camera and other electronic equipment and was assembling it, while I was preparing a box to protect it from the weather. Such a box had to be waterproof, but just how waterproof? In British Columbia, the summers are often beautiful but the winters can be wet. In the past fifteen years, the housing industry has been insulating heavily to avoid heat loss (which is great) but also sealing every possible crack (which is not so great). This lack of air circulation has caused devastating damage through wood rot. With this in mind, my camera box is designed to keep the rain out but let air in.

September 27, 2004 was Eagle Cam Day (EC Day). Jed Young, the arborist was there to climb up the tree with the camera and Doug Wood to string the co-axial cable from the camera to the house. The eagle tree, being eighteen feet around, was almost impossible to climb. Jed had to climb a smaller tree nearby for the first fifty feet, and then swing across to the eagle tree for the remaining climb to the nest at the 120-foot level.

Once in the nest, Jed held the camera in the approximate position for installation and, using his cell phone, called down to the house for instructions. We turned on the TV set where we could see Jed in the nest. Sitting in our living room were Jed's wife, Karen, her parents, two friends of ours from Vancouver, my wife, Sheila, and myself. It was like watching the first man on the moon. Jed's wife had never before seen him so close up in action. "Can you aim it down a bit," I asked, "and more to the left…that's it…spike it there!" The nest was about three and a half feet across on the inside and seven feet across on the outside. Jed could sit in it quite easily. Because of the stories of cats and dogs (or their collars) being found in eagle nests, I asked Jed if there were any cats or dogs. He checked around the nest and held up a variety of bones in front of the camera for us to see. There were fish bones, bird bones and the skull of a mink — but no cats or dogs.

First Pictures

Returning eagles first spotted the new camera. *Photo: Live cam*

Not long after the eagles returned to the nest, they spotted something new — the camera. They stared at it and glared at it as only eagles can do. One of them stepped closer, pecked around the edges of the camera and then pushed its beak into the center of the lens. As the eagle stepped forward it became larger and larger until it looked like a giant staring out of the TV into our room.

A giant eagle staring into our room.

To protect the camera from the weather, it was encased in a plywood box with Plexiglas across the front, acting like a mirror. Our eagles could see their own reflections, which concerned them at first, but in a week or two they took no notice.

The pictures are of breathtaking clarity. The eagles' feathers are a variety of brown shades, each with unique colouration, some an iridescent blue. When it rains you can see the drops combine into larger drops and then into rivulets, running off their backs, not wetting them in the slightest. To see these beautiful birds so clearly is a pleasure in itself.

The male's white head is always immaculately well groomed, while the female's head is dishevelled. They both have crinkly yellow feet, but those of the male are a shade darker. The female, at that time, had two light brown feathers running down the center of her back. These lighter feathers were the older ones, next in

The female is boss of the nest. *Photo: Live Cam*

line for moulting, and are no longer there. None of these things could be seen without the aid of the new camera.

The camera is also a wonderful tool for observing their behaviour. When they first brought branches to the nest, it became obvious that one of them was the boss. This one decided where the branches were to be placed, and threatened the other if it didn't comply. The threat consisted of a pecking motion towards the other's head — a technique, no doubt, perfected as a chick. I taped these activities, showed them around and pointed out the mean nature of the male eagle, assuming that males are always the mean ones (I've been well indoctri-

nated). After one showing, "Maj" Birch, director of a bird rescue center, discreetly suggested that the aggressive eagle might well be the female. Of course, she was right. My first lesson: female eagles are larger, stronger, and more aggressive than males. The males are often under the threat of being "hen-pecked."

Maj Birch of Mountainaire Avian Rescue Society, before releasing a recovered eagle. *Photo: Maj Birch*

The male eagle isn't completely intimidated by the female. Sometimes he brings a stick with the intention of placing it where he wants it to go. She grabs the stick but he refuses to let go, resulting in a tug-of-war, which might last for ten minutes. She'll put the stick on her side of the nest and he'll pull it back to his side. She threatens to peck his head, causing him to step back and so on it goes. The stick generally ends up where she wants it. On one occasion, however, the male reached for the stick when she wasn't looking and placed it back where he wanted it.

Several times we saw the male bring a fish to the nest and begin feeding, only to have the female take it from him and devour it completely herself. Perhaps, for reproductive success, it is more important that the female be well fed. And again, just a few days before she laid an egg the female was reluctant to leave the nest, so the male began bringing herring to her, a consideration he would never have shown at any other time of the year.

Later, when they were taking turns sitting on the eggs, the male displayed remarkable gentleness. He landed on the nest, stepped close to her, picked up a small twig and placed it gently on her back, as if to say, "Here I am. I'll take a turn." She then rose up and he took over. This occurred at least four times.

On warm days, the eagles could be seen nodding off just like humans might do. Their eyelids would slowly drop over their eyes and their heads would sag down, and then suddenly jerk up, eyes opening for a few seconds, only to drop off again — a losing battle against sleep.

The new camera was sensational. It brought the observation of eagles into a totally new dimension. The term "a revolutionary improvement" is not an exaggeration. It gave a personal picture of eagle behaviour, far better than anything I had seen in the previous fifteen years. Rather than seeing the eagles as statistics, they now appeared as individuals, beautiful in appearance, with endlessly interesting behaviour, stead-fastly struggling to bring up their offspring.

The direct emotional impact of this experience is expressed by "Parrotlady" on the Hancock Wildlife Channel: "It showed us a side we never considered and we got to see the companionship, caring and I will say, love, of these two beautiful, graceful old timers…Unforgettable." People often talked of them as Mom and Pop Hornby.

Seen Around the World

At the end of the eagle season, I condensed the tapes down to one thirty-six-minute tape showing the most interesting activities. After enjoying the eagle video with family and friends, I began showing it to other groups of people; first to the local elementary school, then to the seniors' group, and then to a newcomers' club at Qualicum Beach on Vancouver Island. They all enjoyed the eagles immensely.

I then showed my video to serious "eagle" people, members of the Wildlife Tree Stewards. Attending that day was David Hancock, an eagle biologist I had heard about years

ago, but had never met. After the video was over, he stood up and said, "In fifty years of watching eagles, I've never seen such good pictures. Everyone in the world must see these eagles!" I was thrilled that a person of his background and experience would be so complimentary of my first effort. But I wasn't so sure about his second statement, "Everyone in the world must see these eagles!" Quite

David Hancock, who saw the web-cam possibilities, and made it all happen.

an exaggeration, I thought. But the events of the next few months proved he wasn't that far off.

Three days after returning home, I got a phone call from David discussing the possibility of a webcam. I was in favour, as long as someone else paid for it and handled the technology involved. "I'll look after that," he replied. A week later he came to Hornby Island and two weeks later a load of computers and related equipment arrived. David is a man of action, no hesitation here. Just get on with it. The next arrival (on his motorcycle) was Richard Pitt, a computer whiz, specializing in "broadband streaming." He got the system running in the next two weeks, although not without complications and adjustments.

Richard Pitt got the system running.

The signals were then sent from our house to Infotec, the Internet server in Los Angeles. They have equipment that can split the signals from Hornby Island into thousands of signals, equally clear and strong, and transmit them around the world.

I remember the first time the picture was successfully

transmitted. The eagle was in the nest. I turned on my computer and there it was — the eagle. The signals had traveled from our video camera all the way down to Los Angeles and back again to our computer. I felt like Marconi transmitting the first radio signal across the Atlantic. I could see the eagle move in the nest and thirty seconds later, it moved on my computer screen. The delay was caused by the computer translating video signals from the camera into digital signals for transmission. Once that is done, the signals to the world are almost instantaneous.

There were many glitches in the early efforts to send these signals and it was decided to keep the eagle cam address secret until it was working smoothly. One group of bloggers somehow found this address and it was fun to read their comments:

First person starting the topic: "Wow, I found a neat site showing an eagle nest."

Next comment: "Yeah, I saw it too. Cool."

Then: "Where is Hornby Island?"

"Along the east coast, I think."

"It couldn't be. It's daylight where the eagle is and it's now nighttime on the east coast."

"I have an uncle in Vancouver. He says it's just north of there."

"Which is the female?"

"Don't they ever eat?"

In the first day there were fifteen people on this site discussing the eagles. By the fifth day there were several hundred and thereafter it was by far the most discussed topic on their talk line. It struck me that most of the participants were watching the eagles during working hours. Some talked of taking sick leave to watch the eagles. One said he has a special button on his computer, the HCTB button (Here Comes The Boss). When the boss comes, he presses the button and simulated work appears on the screen.

The explosive interest shown by these bloggers was a preview of what was yet to come. The next indication came when I gave the address to my sister-in-law in Melbourne, Australia. We soon received e-mails from her with endless questions about the eagles. I was amazed that she could be watching the eagles behind our house as easily as we could. She handed the address on to twenty friends in Australia, South Africa, England and Switzerland, and they in turn handed on the address to their friends. In addition, I had given the address to other friends who spread it to hundreds of others. Later, I found out that David Hancock, Richard Pitt, Bob Chappell and others had done the same thing.

By the time the official webcam address was made public, there were a million "hits" per day on the eagle site. A few days later there were four million hits, and so on. All kinds of numbers were coming out. It was announced that more people were watching the eagles than the Pope's investiture, which made me feel particularly pleased, perhaps for subconscious reasons. I had been brought up a Protestant — a thing long gone in the mists of time — but early emotions still hang on.

And then the media caught on — phone calls, e-mails, radio, TV, newspapers and magazines from early morning until late at night. A London reporter woke me up with a phone call - at five o'clock in the morning. Knowing full well what time it was here, he apologized, explaining he had a deadline to meet. I was so stunned I probably answered all of his questions. What I should have said was (expletive deleted)! Soon after this, a TV interviewer asked how I was holding up under the barrage. He explained that I was now undergoing what is called "media bombing." I was pulled two ways. It was wonderful that so many people were interested in the eagles, and at the same time I was staggered. Questions, questions, questions all daylong; questions that I was most pleased to answer, but tiring nonetheless.

As the success of the eagle cam became known, there were a number of side effects to deal with. Rumours were now circulating that Hornby Island would be inundated by hordes of people, overloading our ferries, plugging our roads and trampling our gardens — totally disrupting our peaceful island. An extremely agitated person accosted me, "Why did you do this? Why did you say the nest was on Hornby Island?" It had me sputtering. I explained that I had no idea the eagle cam was going to take off like that. "You should have known. You should have thought about it before opening your mouth."

Other stories spread about the amount of money that was being made. When there are a million hits a day, there's big money being made by somebody. Are you getting your share? And then advertising began appearing on the eagle site. This really upset many people. "Can't anything be free from commercialism?" The excitement of the first few days took on a darker aspect. I began to worry that the owners of the eagle tree would think I had deceived them. I had obtained permission to put a camera in their tree so I could learn more about eagles, not for making money. And now there was talk of massive profits. Nobody made a penny on this venture, but that didn't change the talk. It looked as if I had deceived the Ministry of Environment as well. They had trusted me to use the camera for education and science, and now it looked more like a business venture. How did all this happen?

Infotec, the server, had unused capacity on their outgoing server and agreed to transmit the eagle cam pictures at no cost to David Hancock or myself. I looked at this as a wonderful chance to spread the appreciation of eagles, and was exceedingly pleased. I am absolutely convinced that David Hancock was thinking exactly the same. He explained how the tapes of the eagles could be stored and made accessible to universities for scholarly studies and how there could be programs for school use. David, too, was thinking of the webcam in terms of education.

But even education costs money, including education through a webcam, and someone has to pay for it. The high-speed lines cost money to construct and it is the servers who have to pay for the use of the lines. In fact, the more "hits" made on a site, the more the server has to pay. If the server is a cable TV company, it passes on the costs by charging the subscribers for their cable service. In the case of the eagle web cam, those watching the eagles (and you may have been one of them) didn't pay a thing. It was free to the viewers. Having millions of users, then, didn't signify revenue, but ever increasing costs.

To reduce the costs, Infotec was forced to seek out advertisers. Or as some looked at it, the eagles had become commercialized. At that time, with everything happening so rapidly, I was rather confused, and worried in particular, that my integrity had been compromised. I had no intention to deceive the tree owners or the Ministry of Environment. It just seemed to happen. This was a low spot. "There's one thing I can do", I thought. "I can pull the plug, and get back to a simple life of watching eagles and someday, perhaps, writing about them." Or could I? That didn't seem possible either. By this time, Infotec had put big money into buying new equipment and hiring more computer experts and had hardly recovered a penny from advertising. David Hancock had invested significant money in getting the signals from my house to Infotec. I can't pull the plug. I can't leave them stranded. I simply had no choice. I felt like I was being washed down a river, completely out of control and unable to get out.

Fortunately, this downside occurred over a brief period, perhaps for only a week or two. Then my daughter, Judy, told me about the Eagle Forum. "You should look at it," she said. And I did. What a boost! All the nice things people were saying. They thanked David and myself a hundred times over for this opportunity to see the wonderful eagles, diligently caring for their eggs. I now could see things through the eyes of the viewers and what an upside this was, far outweighing previous doubts. The camera gave the viewers an intimate view of the two eagles that few had ever seen before. The eagles turned their eggs with so much care. They walked on their knuckles, talons turned under, to avoid harming the eggs. They settled down on the eggs, with a funny wobbling motion and tucked dry grass around them to keep out the drafts. Such attentive-ness. And this was kept up day after day, through sunshine, pouring rains, or storms.

These things alone were worth watching, but on top of this was a drama turning into a tragedy. Everyone was anticipating the eggs hatching and the growth of the future chicks. The closer to that date, the more people were watching. When the thirty-five-day deadline arrived, the chick in the first egg had not even started pecking a hole in the shell. I then pointed out that last year the egg had taken thirty-eight days to hatch, so there was still hope. Then I thought of all the elementary school students totally wrapped up with the eagles and put out a warning: Eagles' eggs often failed. Be prepared.

On a Sunday night the two eggs were there, but when I turned on my camera early on Monday morning, there was only one egg. I could hardly believe my eyes. Turning on the Forum, the first response was, "There's only one egg!" and many others confirmed the same. I went under the eagle tree, but could find no egg.

We consoled ourselves that one egg was still left — our last hope — but that one was overdue also. We watched and waited, hoping to see the chick peck its way out. We imagined seeing small holes in the egg — almost an "eagle-fever" — but nothing ever happened. A few days later, the eagle got off the egg and it was crushed. I looked around the nest, hoping that a tiny chick had first hatched before the shell had crushed, but there was no such thing. The eagles looked sadly at the empty shell. Later in the day, they came back to sit on the shat-tered egg. The next day they did the same, for the last time, and then gave up. It was over. Just an empty nest.

People were totally moved by the "eagle" experience and expressed such wonderful thoughts on the Forum. A woman in

England told how she had spent the last month with her dying father, brought closer together by watching the eagles. The eagles had portrayed the deeper values of family and dealing with death. A teacher of a special needs class told how her pupils were better able to interrelate with each other and express emotions, brought about by the eagles. Many spoke of it as being a life-changing experience. And what made me exceedingly pleased, hundreds ended their comments with the statement; "We must take better care of our environment." The eagles didn't say a word, but what lessons they taught. They penetrated to the core of our emotions.

I will close by quoting a few of these comments, which have added a deep and lasting joy to my life. I feel so fortunate to have been part of this great event.

Who knew it would matter so much to so many? It did, and in a world struggling with monumental, disastrous issues, these two living creatures have shown us a commitment to life that is breathtaking.

When I was watching with my kids night after night, I would imagine other families sharing the same experience, sharing the same wonder and awe. If it changed us for the better, or motivated us to support wildlife, or even reminded us to spend some time to appreciate the true finer things in life…then we've all truly become richer for the experience.

It also showed that people around the world can all enjoy and appreciate the same thing, regardless of politics or geography or any other boundaries.

From now on when we see an eagle flying by here in Kentucky it won't be just another bird that we enjoy watching. Now we will watch and remember those two beautiful birds who loved their eggs till the bitter end. They would have been such wonderful parents. Thank you. I will never forget mum and pop.

...two of God's creatures that don't even know that their journey has touched and united millions all over the world. How amazing is that!

Hard to express the mix of emotions, as I watched this story unfold, not knowing the ending until the very last page. Fascination, anticipation, Joy, devastation, grief and finally...respect, awe, and acceptance and wonder.

They were teachers... and they'll never know just how much they taught ... to so many around the world.

The Eagle Chicks Did Hatch
by Aonach Dubh

Today the sun was up early and I saw the eagle chicks — all of you — coming into being. The eagles were successful, they gave birth to their children. YOU are their children! For these two birds have, through you, affected the consciousness of man.

The chicks did hatch, and they spread their wings across the whole world, affecting the hearts and minds of millions of humans, who in turn also have the power to affect man's relationship with the natural world.

| Thunder and Lightning. | Lightning wanted to be up there with Thunder, but toppled off again. |

Postscript

After the failed 2006 season, the two eagles stayed in the region for the remainder of the summer. When they migrated in September, Jed, the tree climber, raised the camera a foot higher — necessary because the eagles add another six inches of material to the nest each year. We also installed a second camera, higher up and set farther back, taking in the nest and also the surrounding branches. Thus we would be able to watch the eaglets out on the branches, learning to fly. But the question was always there. Would there ever be more eaglets? The eagles are now quite elderly for the wild.

The cameras were tested and were in perfect positions. I was looking forward to the next season, but a series of winter storms put both cameras out of commission, so I had to go back to observing from the ground, using binoculars and telescope.

In the spring of 2007, the Hornby eagles laid eggs as usual. But would they be fertile? This was answered thirty-five days later when the eagles began bringing fish to the nest. They don't take fish to the nest unless there is a mouth to feed. So one egg at least must have hatched. Five weeks later I spotted a chick for the first time. This was better than last year. After several more weeks, hoping to see a second chick, I finally accepted that there would only be one chick.

Then on July 13 (Friday the 13th), we had a powerful thunderstorm and I checked how the eaglet was managing. Looking through the telescope, I could see it sitting on the edge of the nest, completely unconcerned. It started flapping its wings and to my surprise, a second pair of wings began flapping behind it, appearing to be a single bird with four wings. A miracle...two eaglets! It took me several days and many more sightings to really believe it was true.

After the stormiest winter ever, and having first sighted the two eaglets together during a thunderstorm, it seemed appropriate to name them "Thunder" and "Lightning." Thunder, a female, was larger and more advanced than Lightning, a male. Thunder fledged on July 21, 2007 and Lightning five days later. She migrated north to the salmon rivers on August 19 and Lightning, eight days later — another completed cycle in the lives of the Hornby Island eagles. So, the drama goes on. How long will the Hornby eagles live? Will they have more offspring in future years? I will keep you informed.

Doug Carrick

A Philosophy of Life

At the bottom of page 16, I expressed my feelings about eagles and all the other creatures. "They are all part of this wonderful fabric of life, sharing this same territory."

Artist: Sloane Nixon

As this book was nearing completion, I saw the above picture on the "School Page" of our local "First Edition". It was drawn by Sloane Nixon, 11 years of age, with the caption "We may look different but we are all part of the same world." Exactly how I feel and, I expect, exactly how many of you feel.

Dedicated to Benn Kramer, "The Eagle Man of Hornby Island"

Hornby Island has a population of one thousand people. Some in our small society stand out from the others, and Benn Kramer was one of them. He was the "Eagle Man of Hornby Island." As the caretaker of Bradsdadsland campsite, he became familiar with the eagles nesting there. He climbed a large fir about seventy feet from the nest and spent much time observing his eagles.

Each day he went scuba diving for fish, climbed the tree and fed them to the eagles. They got used to him and would take the fish out of his hand. The hundreds of campers who stayed at Bradsdadsland watched this daily ritual and loved it. It became one of the perks of staying at this campsite.

One summer an eaglet fell out of the nest, as related earlier, and Benn climbed the tree, returning it to the nest. It was a dramatic event that appealed to the media, and soon Benn was featured on several TV programs. He thus became well known, not only to the locals and to the campers at Bradsdadsland, but across Canada.

What struck people more than anything was the way Benn climbed these giant trees — in bare feet and without ropes — quite unnerving to most people. He had found something that he could do that few others would even dare.

And more amazing, Benn was autistic. He had not learned to read until he was eleven years of age. I would say to him, "Are there any eggs yet?" and Benn would repeat, "Any eggs yet?" "Yes, are there any eggs yet?" Conversations often had to be repeated. His brother explained that Benn experienced language just as others would see a poorly functioning TV program, 90 percent "snow" — a terrible barrier to communication. Communication is so important for human happiness, and often people with varying degrees of autism are denied this.

Benn and I met on occasions to talk about eagles and one time he told me he had been feeling depressed. Soon after this, he met an attractive young woman who also had autism. They became engaged and put a deposit on a house. He was so happy, and everyone was happy for him. And then tragedy struck. Benn died in a climbing accident. What had made him so outstanding became his demise. Benn's life was a story of struggle, triumph and tragedy.

I always remember the interviewer on a TV show saying to Benn, "They call you The Eagle Man of Hornby Island." "Yes," said Benn, "The Eagle Man of Hornby Island." His eyes were just gleaming. He was so proud. This is how I remember Benn Kramer.

Hornby Island

Hornby Island, located on the northwestern coast of the Georgia Strait, is two short ferry rides from Vancouver Island. It is six miles long and four miles wide, overlooked by its prominent skyline feature, Mount Geoffrey. There are two outstanding beaches on the island and many lesser beaches, with convenient public access to most of the waterfront. Helliwell Park is our jewel, donated to the island by David Helliwell in 1976 for the perpetual pleasure of locals and visitors alike.

The "Islands Trust," an elected body, regulates Hornby Island, aiming to conserve its rural and natural setting. This is done mainly by limiting the subdivision of agricultural land to lots no smaller than twenty acres, and other property to no less than ten acres. Also helping the "rural and natural setting" is the fact that almost 40 percent of the land has been dedicated to parks. All this is great for birds, deer and other wildlife, and also for humans. The largest parks, which are on Mount Geoffrey, are laced with trails for hiking, biking and horse riding — and great for dogs.

Ferry leaving Denman Island for Hornby Island.

There are only 1,000 permanent residents on Hornby Island, but what a diverse group they are! The families of the original settlers were followed by an influx of hippies and draft-dodgers in the late 1960s and early 70s, some left-wing idealists, visitors who grew to love the non-conforming lifestyles, and many others. There are many artistic people on Hornby Island — painters, potters, weavers, quilters, musicians, dancers, photographers, writers, poets — and an equal diversity of philosophies and lifestyles.

Such a mix of people, all having strongly held opinions,

Tribune Bay.

Helliwell Park (southern tip of Hornby Island).

can be a source of conflict, especially when so many activities are community-based efforts; but most people have learned a high degree of tolerance — live and let live. There are more agreements than disagreements.

We all agree on the conservation of our natural habitat. The forests of Mount Geoffrey are looked at not as a commodity to be logged, but as nature's way of managing our precious water supply, preventing immediate runoff and erosion. We are enthusiastic recyclers and are proud of our recycling depot, which was a pioneer in British Columbia. Part of this depot is the "Free Store" where people drop off clothes, furniture, books, TV sets, and so on. Those who can use these items just help themselves.

We all chose to come to Hornby Island and are proud of our lifestyles. A lot of eagles have also chosen to live on Hornby, because of the number of suitable trees for nesting, because of the beaches and the sea, and because it is uncluttered with people. A great place to live — both for people and eagles.

The Hornby Island community hall.

Eagle Dates — Hornby Island

Return from Migration October 2

Major Nest Building Time From October 20 to November 15. Bringing branches to nest — large ones around the outside and fine twigs on the inside.

Winter Survival Time November 15 to February 15. With shorter and colder days, nest-building stops. Much of their time is now spent getting food, mostly fish but also winter-weakened birds and ducks.

Mating Think of St Valentine's Day, February 14 (a suitable time for mating) — but include the two weeks before and after this date — in other words, the whole month of February. Eagles are also seen mating in the first half of March, just a week or two before laying eggs. But at no other times in the year.

Final Nest Preparation A second flurry of nest-preparation takes place from mid-February to mid-March — adding more branches, followed by soft materials like dry grass and moss.

Egg Laying March 25. A second egg 3 or 4 days later.

Brooding The male and female take turns sitting on the eggs for approximately 35 days — from March 25 to May 1. One could consider the month of April as the "brooding" month.

Chicks Hatch May 1.

Chick Development Peeps can be heard by June 10
Sitting on edge of nest by June 20
Flapping wings by June 25
Flapping and Jumping by July 10

First Flight July 25. (85 days after hatching)

Migration Off Island Mid-August. This migration includes adults, new eaglets and any other non-breeding eagles. All eagles go. Eagles with no eaglets may leave two weeks earlier. Eagles with late-hatching or slower developing eaglets may leave two weeks later. A large variation on this date.

Adult Eagles (Only) Return to Island October 2. Only a few days variation on this date.

Immatures Straggle Back to Island One or two arrive back in November, a few in December and increasing numbers in the next few months.

Dates will be earlier in southern Vancouver Island, the Fraser Valley and further South. Dates will be later in northern Vancouver Island and up the coast to Alaska. All dates shown here are subject to variations - a guide only.

Doug Carrick — at home, 2003.
Photo: Kevin Hatt

About the Author

Doug Carrick and his wife, Sheila, have owned their Hornby Island property for twenty-seven years and have been retired there for fifteen years. Having the eagle family begin nesting behind their house opened up a new interest, and being a retired accountant, Doug was compelled to keep accurate records.

He had thought of writing a book on these eagles earlier, but spent too much time watching them in the cameras installed in the tree. In the winter of 2006/2007, however, severe storms knocked out the cameras, and that turned out to be a blessing. — "It's an ill wind that blows no good." — It enabled him to devote the winter to writing this book.

NOTES:
Compare your own observations from year to year.

_____

_____

_____

_____

_____

_____

_____

_____

_____

_____

_____

_____

_____

_____

_____

_____

_____

_____

_____

110

Coming in Fall 2008

hancock house

Benn Kramer: Eagle Man of Hornby Island
David Hancock with photography by Benn Kramer
978-0-88839-640-2
8½ x 11, sc, 96 pages

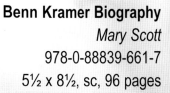

Benn Kramer Biography
Mary Scott
978-0-88839-661-7
5½ x 8½, sc, 96 pages

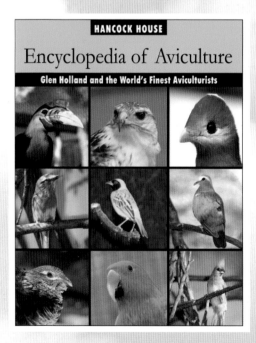